Teaching Public Administration Creatively

INSTRUCTOR'S RESOURCE MANUAL

to accompany

PUBLIC ADMINISTRATION: CONCEPTS AND CASES

EIGHTH EDITION

RICHARD J. STILLMAN II

University of Colorado at Denver

HOUGHTON MIFFLIN COMPANY   BOSTON   NEW YORK

Sponsoring Editor: Katherine Meisenheimer
Assistant Editor: Christina Lembo
Editorial Assistant: Jake Perry
Assistant Manufacturing Coordinator: Priscilla Bailey
Senior Marketing Manager: Nicola Poser

Printed in the U.S.A.

ISBN: 0-618-31046-0

123456789-QF-08 07 06 05 04

Contents

PART ONE

Course Preparation and Teaching Methods

Memo 1

TO: Fellow Public Administration Teachers

FROM: RJS

SUBJECT: On Teaching Public Administration

It is not easy to teach public administration, or to teach anything today for that matter. We college teachers face many competing demands on our time: We serve on faculty committees, advise student groups, address alumni groups, confer with deans, offer professional seminars, prepare for courses, grade mountains of papers and exams, and still try to keep a few minutes free to sandwich in some library research. Cost-conscious college administrators push us to "produce" more; and students press us at the same time to be more accessible as role models, serious scholars, personal advisers, and classroom entertainers. And those of us in public administration, public affairs, or government education usually are expected to render special services, such as professional consulting, advising, and developmental activities, to the communities where we live. Along with all of these responsibilities, we must devote at least some of our time to the intellectual and scholarly advancement of our field. Certainly it is hard to do many things at once and to do them well, or at least as well as we'd like.

Yet I think most of us continue to teach public affairs, public administration, or government because we find the job especially challenging and rewarding. Awakening students to public issues and problems can be fulfilling. Short-term field assignments—helping to design a citizen survey for a local parks and recreation department or contributing to a staff-development course on effective administrative decision-making techniques—can give special insight into governmental processes and problems. This kind of work also offers the stimulation of being personally involved in public problems, an experience that few other

3

academics encounter. Most of us who teach in the field believe that public administration is central to improving our society; so plying our trade yields personal
satisfaction, even if few outsiders fully appreciate what we do.

Obviously I believe that public administration is an exciting and worthwhile enterprise. Participating in it and teaching it combine fun and virtue.
Almost thirty years ago, I undertook to prepare the first edition of *Public
Administration: Concepts and Cases.* My aim was to communicate the field's
special qualities to new students. Frankly, I wrote the text because I was dissatis-
fied (as I still am) with most textbooks available in the field. I was irritated by
their superficial rendering of complex subject matter, their insensitivity to the
realities of administrative processes, and their failure to engage students in the
challenging contemporary problems that involve public administration. I felt the
need to educate students in the field more creatively. Public administration is
much more interesting and useful to know than many unimaginative texts make it
seem.

In an effort to do better, I began experimenting with various approaches and
hit on the "concept-case" approach. This method introduces students systematically to the major concepts and ideas that shape the field today, as written,
mainly, by some of the field's intellectual leaders. Then contemporary case
studies that are both insightful and well written illustrate the key aspects of the
concepts under review. I believe that the concept-case approach gives a sound
understanding of both the theory and the practice of public administration; and it
allows students to see the interconnections among concepts, draw their own conclusions, and generate thought-provoking dialogue. The approach has worked well,
at least for my classes, and seems to be popular now with many of you, my teaching
colleagues. *Public Administration: Concepts and Cases,* currently in its eighth
edition, was ranked by a recent survey of public administration teachers as one of
the top three texts in the field. The height of flattery is that I now see other texts
using the concept-case approach.

I have prepared this guidebook as a companion to the eighth edition of the
text. I prefer, though, not to offer the usual instructor's manual fare of standard-
ized exams, simplistic lecture notes, and uninspired pedagogical suggestions.
Instead, I'd like to share some ideas with you that can help you teach more
creatively using *Public Administration: Concepts and Cases,* Eighth Edition.
Although you may already be teaching with the text very successfully, you might
also like to know what the author has learned while using the concept-case
approach to teach more than fifty introductory public administration courses.

I hope that some of my thoughts can help you improve your teaching effectiveness in introductory classes. What follows, then, is a series of personal memos
about various aspects of introductory course development, from planning (Memo 2)
to the final examination (Memo 15).

Remember that teaching is a highly individualized activity: What works
well for me may fail for you. Read the following memos with a critical eye but an
open and experimental mind. Then decide for yourself whether you want to adopt
any of the suggestions. I encourage you to disagree with what I recommend and to

invent better approaches. To do better at teaching public administration, we must fully exercise our imagination and creativity.

As a postscript, I should add that the following memos advise how to use *Public Administration: Concepts and Cases*, Eighth Edition, as the main classroom text. If you use it to supplement a more standard text, as I know many of you do, the topic index at the beginning of the text offers suggestions for relating individual concepts and cases to particular themes and topics. In addition, the following charts directly compare my text with six other popular public administration texts. I've listed the specific readings and case studies that shed special light on each chapter of each book. Remember that this is a partial list: Many cases in *Public Administration: Concepts and Cases* illustrate a number of important administrative ideas.

Rosenbloom, *Public Administration*, 6/e	Stillman, *Public Administration: Concepts and Cases*, 8/e
Chapter 1	Reading 1; Case Study 1
Chapter 2	Reading 2; Case Study 2
Chapter 3	Reading 5; Case Study 5
Chapter 4	Readings 2, 10, and 15; Case Studies 2, 10, and 15
Chapter 5	Readings 6, 7, and 11; Case Studies 6, 7, and 11
Chapter 6	Reading 12; Case Studies 12 and 13
Chapter 7	Reading 8; Case Study 8
Chapter 8	Reading 13; Study 13
Chapter 9	Case Studies 1, 2, 5, 10, and 16
Chapter 10	Readings 14 and 16; Case Studies 1, 3, 5, 13, and 16
Chapter 11	Readings 1 and 3; Case Studies 1 and 3
Chapter 12	Readings 14 and 16; Case Studies 14 and 16
Chapter 13	Reading 1; Case Study 1

Starling, *Managing the Public Sector*, 6/e	Stillman, *Public Administration: Concepts and Cases*, 8/e
Chapter 1	Reading 6; Case Study 6
Chapter 2	Reading 1; Case Study 1
Chapter 3	Reading 5; Case Study 5
Chapter 4	Reading 16; Case Study 16
Chapter 5	Reading 3; Case Study 3

Chapter 6	Readings 8 and 9; Case Studies 8 and 9
Chapter 7	Readings 2 and 10; Case Studies 2 and 10
Chapter 8	Readings 10 and 11; Case Studies 10 and 11
Chapter 9	Reading 13; Case Study 13
Chapter 10	Readings 6 and 10; Case Studies 6 and 10
Chapter 11	Reading 12; Case Study 12
Chapter 12	NA

Henry, *Public Administration and Public Affairs*, 9/e	Stillman, *Public Administration: Concepts and Cases*, 8/e
Chapter 1	Reading 2; Case Study 2
Chapter 2	Reading 1; Case Study 1
Chapters 3–5	Readings 3, 6, 7, 10, and 11; Case Studies 3, 6, 7, 10, and 11
Chapter 6	Reading 10; Case Study 10
Chapter 7	Reading 13; Case Study 13
Chapter 8	Reading 12; Case Study 12
Chapter 9	Readings 6 and 11; Case Studies 6 and 11
Chapter 10	Readings 8 and 13; Case Studies 8 and 13
Chapter 11	Reading 15; Case Study 15
Chapter 12	Reading 5; Case Study 5
Chapter 13	Reading 16; Case Study 16

Milakovich and Gordon, *Public Administration in America,* 8/e	Stillman, *Public Administration: Concepts and Cases,* 8/e
Chapter 1	Reading 1; Case Study 1
Chapter 2	Reading 3; Case Study 3
Chapter 3	Readings 4 and 14; Case Studies 4 and 14
Chapter 4	Reading 5; Case Study 5
Chapter 5	Reading 10; Case Study 10
Chapter 6	Reading 8; Case Study 8
Chapter 7	Reading 7; Case Study 7
Chapter 8	Readings 6 and 11; Case Studies 6 and 11
Chapter 9	Reading 12; Case Study 12
Chapter 10	Reading 10; Case Study 10
Chapter 11	Case Studies 1, 2, 9, 14, and 16
Chapter 12	Case Studies 3, 6, 7, 12, and 15

Denhardt, *Public Administration: An Action Orientation,* 4/e	Stillman, *Public Administration: Concepts and Cases,* 8/e
Chapter 1	Reading 1; Case Study 1
Chapter 2	Readings 2, 4, and 14; Case Studies 2, 4, and 14
Chapter 3	Reading 5; Case Study 5
Chapter 4	Reading 16; Case Study 16

Chapter 5	Reading 5; Case Study 5
Chapter 6	Readings 6, 7, and 11; Case Studies 6 and 11
Chapter 7	Reading 13; Case Study 13
Chapter 8	Readings 8, 9, and 10; Case Studies 8, 9, and 10
Chapter 9	Case Studies 3, 14, and 15
Chapter 10	Readings 6, 9, and 11; Case Studies 6, 9, and 11
Chapter 11	Readings 6 and 11; Case Studies 6 and 11
Chapter 12	Readings 14, 15, and 16; Case Studies 14, 15, and 16

Shafritz/Russell, *Introducing Public Administration*, 4/e	Stillman, *Public Administration: Concepts and Cases*, 8/e
Chapter 1	Reading 1; Case Study 1
Chapter 2	Readings 3 and 4; Case Studies 3 and 4
Chapter 3	Reading 2; Case Study 2
Chapter 4	Reading 5; Case Study 5
Chapter 5	Reading 16; Case Study 16
Chapter 6	Readings 8, 9, and 10; Case Studies 8, 9, and 10
Chapter 7	Readings 6, 7, 9, 10, and 11; Case Studies 6, 8, and 11
Chapter 8	Reading 10; Case Study 10
Chapter 9	Case Studies 3, 5, 11, and 15
Chapter 10	Case Studies 3, 5, 8, 11, and 14
Chapter 11	Readings 7 and 11; Case Study 11

Chapter 12   Readings 2 and 3; Case Studies 2 and 3

Chapter 13   Reading 12; Case Study 12

Chapter 14   Reading 15; Case Study 15

Memo 2

TO: Fellow Public Administration Teachers

FROM: RJS

SUBJECT: The Syllabus

It is said Alfred Hitchcock committed each of his movie scripts to memory before he began shooting the film. He memorized all the details of set design, actors' staging, costumes, even intonation. In this way, Hitchcock felt he could focus on the angle of the camera lens rather than on the script page. His concentration on the audience's angle of vision led to thrillers like *Psycho*, *The Birds*, and *North by Northwest*.

I don't intend to suggest that you should memorize every lecture before stepping into class; but like a film director, an instructor should have a good script and be familiar with it. A well-designed syllabus—detailed and carefully developed—very likely leads to a successful course. This kind of syllabus serves as a plan that determines what is going to happen in class. Designing it forces you to think about course objectives and class procedures, and to do so systematically. And it spells out the course's content and requirements clearly, carefully, and accurately for the students, who deserve to know ahead of time what the course's objectives are, what is going to happen in class, and what the instructor expects them to do.

The following is a sample syllabus for an undergraduate introductory public administration class. I compiled it myself and have used it regularly with success. Notice its major elements:

1. The heading lists the course title, number, section, and department and the time of year the class is given.

2. The first four or five lines indicate the instructor's name, phone, email and office number, class hours, and office hours.

3. Required and optional texts are identified so that the students can obtain them quickly from the bookstore. I always put some copies on library reserve for those who cannot afford to purchase them.

4. Next the syllabus *briefly* describes the course and its objectives. Students should know what sort of academic field they're getting into so that they can tell in the first class whether they might be interested.

5. The syllabus then describes the course's organization, covering such points as the mode of teaching (lectures, seminars, or whatever), grading procedures, any required written or oral reports, and the nature of examinations.

6. The remaining pages of the syllabus indicate the specific readings and case studies used in each segment and the timing of exams and reports (use specific dates if possible). I also include a short paragraph about the material, and I raise issues for students to think about before they begin reading the material. I always use the first session to describe the syllabus and the course in some detail for the students (see Memo 6). The specifics of each segment of the course are discussed in subsequent memos. For now, notice how the segments are broken down and the time allotted to each. This timing obviously varies according to the interests of the instructor and the number of classes in a quarter or semester. Also, there are no hard-and-fast rules on what content *should* be covered; but I like to give students who are new to the field a broad overview of its scope and substance, its historical development, its management and personnel practices, and its budgetary and fiscal management systems.

A wise teacher plans slack time into a course. There should be room to adjust the pace to the students' abilities, special topical interests, and the opportunity for a guest speaker or field trip. New teachers often try to cover too much in one course and then, running out of time, hurry through too much material in too short a time at the end. A teacher needs room to maneuver. Don't be afraid to leave out some things, add topics that interest you, or change your tempo.

Sample Syllabus for Undergraduates

INTRODUCTION TO PUBLIC ADMINISTRATION

Government 241—Sections 1 & 2

Public Affairs Department
Fall 2004

Lecturer:	Richard Stillman
Phone:	323-2064, 323-2272 (secretary)
Email:	Richard.Stillman@cudenver.edu
Office:	Robinson Hall, Room 2260
Class hours:	Section 1—Tuesday/Thursday 3:00–4:15 P.M.
	Section 2—Thursday 7:20–10:00 P.M.
Office hours:	One hour before and after class and by appointment

Required Texts (Both texts have been placed on library reserve.)

Richard J. Stillman, *The American Bureaucracy*, 3rd ed. (Belmont, CA: Wadsworth, 2004), paperback.

Richard J. Stillman, *Public Administration: Concepts and Cases*, 8th ed. (Boston: Houghton Mifflin, 2005), paperback.

Course Description and Objectives

Public administration involves the "core activities" of government that are performed, for the most part, by highly trained experts and specialized organizations; its purpose is the development and implementation of public policy. This broad definition encompasses a large dynamic portion of government at all three levels of the federal system, engaging even nonprofit and private enterprise.

It is impossible to cover in one course all of the material from the academic discipline of public administration; it is even less reasonable to attempt to develop every skill that is necessary to be an effective public manager. Therefore, this course attempts to familiarize you with the various complexities of the field of public administration—other courses are offered that allow you to continue your study and increase your skills. All students of government, whatever their focus, need to be cognizant of the tremendous importance of public administration and administrators within the political system. This course is designed to provide you with an introduction to public administration through readings, cases, discussion, and practical exercises.

Course Organization

Although this is primarily a lecture course, students are expected to join in class discussion, and class participation is part of the grade. Students are expected also to have read the assigned material *before* it is discussed in class.

As the course progresses, I hope to get to know each member of the class by name and to deal with your individual difficulties with the class. *But I cannot help resolve your problems unless you tell me about them.* So please stop by my office during office hours to discuss any academic troubles.

Grading

The grade for the semester is based on the following criteria:

- Midterm exam: 25%
- Final exam (cumulative): 30%
- Written report: 25%
- Class participation, oral report: 20%

Exams are essay and short answer, but predominately essay. You will be given a choice of questions (for example, three or four out of five questions). *An exam cannot be made up unless you notify me, before the time of the exam, that you cannot take it and you have a reasonable excuse.*

The class participation grade is based on the following:

- Participation in general class discussion
- Presentation of a specific class oral exercise assigned during the semester

Written Report

The written report is a team research project on a major local issue. You are expected to deliver your findings orally in class (on a panel with others studying the same local issue) as well as in a written report. Time will be provided *in class* for your research.

You must choose and secure my approval of your topic by the second week of class, and the paper is due no later than the last week of class. Late papers will be marked down one grade (an A paper will receive a B). Term paper format is expected to meet the standards described by Campbell, Turabian, or similar term paper manuals. Spelling, punctuation, and grammar will be considered in assigning the term paper grade. All papers must be *typed*.

Weekly Reading Assignments
"Order of March"

1ST WEEK: INTRODUCTION, ORIENTATION, ASSIGNMENTS

1ST AND 2ND WEEKS: WHAT IS PUBLIC ADMINISTRATION?

Readings: Stillman, *The American Bureaucracy,* Chapter 1
                             Wilson, "The Study of Public Administration," in
                                 Stillman, *PA,* Chapter 1
Case Study: Martin, "The Blast in Centralia No. 5," in Stillman,
                                 PA, Chapter 1

In the first week, we examine the following issues: According to Wilson, why should a study of public administration be developed in America? The sources for its development? Purposes? What is public administration? Does "public" differ from "private" administration according to Wilson and Stillman? What is the role of administration in modern society?

"The Blast in Centralia No. 5" focuses on several issues in modern administration. Queries: Who was responsible for the violent deaths of 111 miners in Centralia, Illinois? How could the disaster have been prevented? What does this case say about the definition, role, and function of public administration in society?

2ND WEEK: THE DEVELOPMENT OF AMERICAN
BUREAUCRACY AND THE PUBLIC SERVICE: AN
HISTORICAL OVERVIEW

Readings: Stillman, *The American Bureaucracy,* Chapter 2
Weber, "Bureaucracy," in Stillman, *PA,* Chapter 2
Madison, *Federalist Paper No. 51* (handout)
U.S. Constitution (handout)

Case Study: Lardner, "How Kristin Died," in Stillman, *PA,*
              Chapter 2

3RD WEEK: THE KEY "INPUTS" INTO PUBLIC
ADMINISTRATION IN AMERICA

Readings: Stillman, *The American Bureaucracy,* Chapter 3
Gaus, "Ecology," in Stillman, *PA,* Chapter 3
Long, "Power and Administration," in Stillman, *PA,*
              Chapter 4
O'Toole, "American Intergovernmental Relations," in
              Stillman, *PA,* Chapter 5

Case Study: Riccucci, "Dr. Helene Gayle and the AIDS Epidemic," in
              Stillman, *PA,* Chapter 3

These next two weeks of readings focus on the growth and external influences that affect the American public service. Queries: What are the reasons for growth observers see in the development of public service? From your reading of the U.S. Constitution, where is the subject of administration mentioned? How did the Founders' conception of the Constitution (reflected in Madison's arguments in *Federalist Paper No. 51*) influence the evolution of American public administration? How does the historical growth of American bureaucracy (see Stillman's *The American Bureaucracy,* Chapter 2) square with either Weber's or Gaus's conceptions of bureaucracy? What does the case study, "Dr. Helene Gayle and the AIDS Epidemic," indicate about the nature of modern American bureaucracy? What critical inputs influence the direction, size, and scope of American bureaucracy today, as well as the creation of bureaucracy?

4TH AND 5TH WEEKS:	ALTERNATIVE METHODS OF MANAGEMENT IN GOVERNMENT

Readings: Stillman, *The American Bureaucracy*, Chapter 5
Rainey and Steinbauer, "Galloping Elephants," in
Stillman, *PA*, Chapter 10

Case Study: Nagel, "The MOVE Disaster," in Stillman, *PA*,
Chapter 8

The fourth and fifth weeks deal with public management as well as organization and management concepts and specifically what is effective management, according to Rainey and Steinbauer, in the public service. What is the best approach? Why? Based on your experience, could you develop a more effective approach to managing government? Explain how *your* ideas on effective methods of public management might have avoided the problems apparent in the case, "The MOVE Disaster."

6TH WEEK:	MIDTERM EXAMINATION

A review will be scheduled ahead of time for this exam. Please come prepared with *your questions.*

7TH WEEK:	A CLOSER LOOK AT THE KEY ELEMENTS OF PUBLIC SERVICE MANAGEMENT: DECISION MAKING, PLANNING, COMMUNICATIONS, AND IMPLEMENTATION

Readings: Lindblom, "The Science of 'Muddling Through,'" in
Stillman, *PA*, Chapter 8
Garnett, "Administrative Communication," in Stillman,
PA, Chapter 9
Matland, "Synthesizing the Implementation
Literature," in Stillman, *PA*, Chapter 13

Case Study: Rosegrant, "The Shootings at Columbine High School,"
in Stillman, *PA*, Chapter 9

This section of the course looks at public service management in closer detail, especially the critical elements of decision making, communications, planning, and implementation. Various models and designs for each of these aspects of management are examined and discussed. The debate between "rational" and "nonrational" approaches is presented, along with the contributions of Charles Lindblom and others to our understanding of administrative activities.

Looking at the case study, "The Shootings at Columbine High School," what decision-making, communicating, planning, and implementation methods were utilized in the case? Were they ineffective, in your opinion? How might they have been improved?

8TH WEEK:	INSIDE PUBLIC ADMINISTRATION AND FIVE SUBSYSTEMS OF PUBLIC PERSONNEL
Readings:	Stillman, *The American Bureaucracy*, Chapter 4 (or Stillman, *PA*, Chapter 7) Wise, "The Public Service Culture," in Stillman, *PA*, Chapter 11
Case Study:	Sontag, "Who Brought Bernadine Healy Down?" in Stillman, *PA*, Chapter 11

This part of the course looks inside bureaucracy to consider five subsystems of public servants who decisively help shape public policy. The case study emphasizes the complex personnel issues arising in professional career systems, specifically for an individual who rose to the top of the Red Cross. Queries: What does the case study indicate about the modern complexities of professional personnel in the public setting? What were the forces behind the issues raised by the case? Could the problems in this case study have been averted? If so, how? Does the Wise reading offer some specific answers to contemporary problems of public personnel motivation?

9TH WEEK:	GUEST SPEAKERS

Please let me know your interests in hearing outside lecturers.

10TH WEEK:	PUBLIC FINANCE AND BUDGETING: TYPES OF BUDGETS, THE BUDGETARY CYCLE, FISCAL POLICY, AND THE POLITICS OF THE BUDGETARY PROCESS
Readings:	Rubin, "The Politics of Public Budgets," in Stillman, *PA*, Chapter 12 Stillman, *The American Bureaucracy*, Chapter 5
Case Study:	Conant, "Wisconsin's Budget Deficit," in Stillman, *PA*, Chapter 12

Perhaps the most controversial and enduring problem of public administration is the choice over the allocation of scarce fiscal resources: Should monies be spent abroad for Middle East aid or domestically for the cities, mass transit, or highways? Frequently these hard choices are determined and implemented within the realm of public finance and the budgetary process. Queries: How are public budgets prepared? What is a public budget? What does Rubin mean by the phrase "clusters of budget decisions"? From your reading of the case study, "Wisconsin's Budget Deficit," how does politics affect budgetary decisions?

11TH–13TH WEEKS: STUDENT REPORTS

14TH WEEK: PRESENT AND FUTURE TRENDS IN PUBLIC
              ADMINISTRATION

Readings: Stillman, *The American Bureaucracy*, Chapters 6 and 7
               Heclo, "Issue Networks," in Stillman, *PA*, Chapter 14
               Wilson, "Bureaucracy and the Public Interest," in
                    Stillman, *PA*, Chapter 15
               Waldo, "Public Administration and Ethics," in
                    Stillman, *PA*, Chapter 16
Case Study: Sims, "Reinventing School Lunch," in Stillman, *PA*,
                    Chapter 14

LAST WEEK: FINAL EXAMINATION

A review session will be held ahead of time. Again, please come prepared with any questions.

Memo 3

TO: Fellow Public Administration Teachers

FROM: RJS

SUBJECT: Oral and Written Reports

The sample syllabus in Memo 2 shows that I am a believer in the written and oral team project. You may not agree with this pedagogical device, but consider what I say here and then decide if you would like to give it a try.

Most undergraduates, and many graduates for that matter, have never worked in public administration. Many have never seen or experienced firsthand the workings of big organizations. So I favor simulating these sorts of work experiences in class in an effort to provide a slice of administrative reality. Simulations are really a form of practice, and practice is essential to the making of an effective administrator in government.

I specifically like team projects because they simulate what goes on in real-world public administration. Unlike academic projects, government projects are rarely carried out and written up by one individual. Most are handled by task forces and other teams. I feel strongly that students in public administration should be exposed to this type of activity—to the difficulties and rewards of working together with various kinds of people.

As a teacher, you may wonder how to judge individual students' performance on team projects, how to grade fairly. I simply ask each team member to identify clearly on the written report what he or she contributed to it. In oral presentations, it is fairly easy to tell what each student has contributed.

I feel that oral and written team projects offer students (1) a unique sense of involvement and participation in the class; (2) an understanding of some of the practical problems of contemporary administration; (3) unusually rewarding opportunities to speak and write; (4) experience in working on a team; (5) practice in field research; (6) a chance to share their research with one another; and (7) a chance to get to know their classmates. Some students have told me that the team project is the best part of my course.

However, team projects *must* be well structured and supervised by the instructor if they are going to work successfully. Careful instructions from the outset are essential. Two sample team projects that I have used follow. (Either one can be attached to the sample syllabus in Memo 2.) In the first one, the Special Student Task Force memo, you appoint several student task forces to investigate major community issues for the city council. Several such issues are listed in the memo, but you can use any topics of local concern. I usually hand this memo to students on the first day of class and give them until the second week of class to select two subjects they would like to work on. In the second week of class I team them up with others interested in the same community issues. I meet with the teams early in the semester to get them started in the right direction with their research. I try to point them toward appropriate field interviews and published material and guide them in how to prepare their oral and written reports. I usually allow two or three weeks at the end of the semester for these 20- to 30-minute team reports. I try to help students organize their presentations, and I encourage them to use slides, charts, and other visual aids to report their findings. By presenting diverse topics, these student task forces can give the class a good overview of several community problems and administrative issues.

The second sample project, the Professions in Government oral and written reports, is meant to get the student teams to examine job opportunities in the public sector. For this project, I suggest that students use the optional text, *Professions in Government,* to pick their topics. This text outlines the nature, roles, activities, power, and other aspects of a dozen important professional groups in government. (Examples are the police, city managers, and educational administrators.) Again, I give students until the second week of class to select the professional group they would like to study. I also ask for a second choice to make it easier to team them up with others interested in exploring the same professional group. And I try to meet with the student teams early in the semester to guide them in their field of research.

This project helps students understand the problems and prospects of public-sector work, and the group reports at the end of the course provide a good overview of contemporary public service. In addition, I have found that this assignment is very appealing to career-minded students. And many students get so involved with their research that they become strong proponents of the professional group they are studying.

Sample Team Project 1

TO: The Special Student Task Force

FROM: Richard Stillman

SUBJECT: Task Force Project Assignment

Your Special Student Task Force is asked to prepare a report for the city council on one of the following issues confronting the city:

Dealing with the homeless

The community drug problem

City transportation facilities

Air pollution

Community parks and recreation

Utilization of computers in
  government

Crime and its control

Public health facilities

Minority employment opportunities

Improving community housing

Alternatives for stimulating the local
  economy

Upgrading public education

Minority discrimination

The local redevelopment programs

Poverty in the city

Issues of special districts

The problems of annexation

Water quality

Public relations in the public sector

Human resource problems in the public
  services

State-local relationships

Administration of the municipal
  courts

Improving the prison system

Public library administration

Local revenues and expenditures

The city planning process

The welfare system in the city

College administration

Local unions and collective bargaining
  in the public sector

Property taxes

Urban renewal

Intergovernmental relations at the
  local level

Waste management

Zoning and land use

The specifics and organization of the report are left to your discretion; however, it should contain the following:

- A short description of the problem under study

- An overview of the present situation in regard to the problem
- The resources and constraints (for example, social, political, or economic) in dealing with the problem
- An outline of the alternative courses of action
- An evaluation of each alternative
- The task force's specific recommendations for dealing with the problem at hand
- A dissenting task force opinion (if necessary)

Your report will be presented to the class in both oral and written form in the eleventh through fourteenth weeks of the course. The oral report should be limited to 30 minutes and will be open to questions. Visual aids may be used in the oral presentation. The written report (limited to 30 pages) should reflect team effort and should be typewritten, with a selected bibliography and footnotes where appropriate.

I cannot stress enough the value of this assignment. Thorough research, field interviews, and creative thinking are essential. Feel free to seek my advice and help. Good luck!

Sample Team Project 2

INSTRUCTIONS FOR PREPARING
THE "PROFESSIONS IN GOVERNMENT"
ORAL AND WRITTEN REPORTS

1. Select your first and second choices of professional groups that you would like to study during the course. A careful review of the Mosher and Stillman text, *Professions in Government*, can help you make your selection from important public professions, such as law, accounting, engineering, military service, city management, foreign service, police, public health management, and teaching.

2. The instructor will ask you for your choices by the second week of class and will team you up with two to six other individuals interested in studying the same profession. You will be given time in class to meet and organize your research efforts.

3. Members of your panel are expected to begin their research right away. An oral report to the entire class is due sometime during the last three weeks of the semester, and a written report is due the last week of class.

4. Panel members should divide the work for both the oral and written presentations fairly among themselves. Be certain to cover the six major portions of the study:

   Part 1: *An overview of the professional group.* What are its purposes? Goals? Role in government? Size? Structure? Activities? Organization? Ideas?

   Part 2: *Historical development.* How did the profession begin? Grow? Evolve? How has it changed over time in terms of size? Functions? Purposes? Ideals? Activities?

   Part 3: *Involvement in public policy.* How does the professional group influence the development and direction of public policy? What are its sources of power and influence? Its limitations in playing policy roles? What groups within the profession exercise the most control and power?

Part 4: *Career opportunities.* What are the current job opportunities in the profession for college graduates? What are the entry levels and career ladders? What are the top positions? How are they reached?

Part 5: *Ideal educational preparation.* What is the best training for the profession? What types of schools should be attended? What courses and degrees are needed? Are advanced training "in-service," special examinations, or membership in professional associations required?

Part 6: *Present and future prospects.* What are the present and future prospects for the professional group? What factors will influence its short- and long-term size? Its salaries? Its power? Its growth? Will it offer a good career in the future for college graduates?

5. In researching these issues, panel members are expected to draw on up-to-date books, articles, and government publications. They also should interview members of the professional group.

6. The oral presentation, which is due between the eleventh and thirteenth weeks of the course, should (a) reflect a coordinated, well-organized team effort; (b) cover all of the points mentioned above about the professional group under examination; (c) have appropriate charts, graphs, and illustrations of major points; (d) include ample preparation to answer questions from the class about the presentation; and (e) show overall imagination and effectiveness in oral delivery. The instructor will carefully critique each panel's presentation after the report.

7. A typewritten report of no more than 30 pages will be due the last week of class. The written report should reflect team effort (that is, do *not* hand in individual papers), but each individual's contribution to the report should be clearly identified. The report must be typewritten, using the proper format for footnotes and bibliography.

8. This assignment has several purposes, but four of the most important follow:

   • It should give you a good overview of professional career opportunities in public service today.
   • It should help you polish your research, writing, and speaking skills.
   • It should help you learn to work effectively on committee assignments.
   • It should give you a chance to study firsthand the power of professionals in modern government.

Memo 4

TO: Fellow Public Administration Teachers

FROM: RJS

SUBJECT: About Teaching Graduate Students

Because they are advanced students, more should be expected from graduate students than from undergraduates. Hence their introductory course should be more demanding.

The following are examples of additional requirements that might be added to an introductory public administration course for graduate students:

1. There should be more readings, particularly theoretical and primary materials.
2. Graduate students ought to be prepared to participate a lot more in discussions in the classroom; that is, the class should be more of a seminar than a lecture course.
3. The written report should be more scholarly. Here I favor firsthand investigation of major public documents in public administration that give students a sense of the historical development of modern public administration institutions and processes. The specifics of this assignment are carefully detailed in the sample syllabus that follows, and the basic documents are all available in the two volumes that are cited in the syllabus—Mosher, *Basic Documents of American Public Administration: 1776–1950,* and Stillman, *Basic Documents of American Public Administration Since 1950.* Again, careful instructor direction is important to the success of this project.

Sample Syllabus for Graduate Students

THEORY AND PRACTICE OF PUBLIC ADMINISTRATION

PUAD 502—Sections 1 & 2

Public Affairs Department
Fall 2004

Lecturer:	Richard Stillman
Phone:	323-2064, 323-2272 (secretary)
Email:	Richard.Stillman@cudenver.edu
Office:	Robinson Hall, Room 2260
Class hours:	Section 1—Monday 4:30–7:10 P.M., Metro Campus 301
	Section 2—Tuesday 7:20–10:00 P.M., Robinson 2230
Office hours:	One hour before and after class and by appointment

Required Texts (All texts have been placed on library reserve.)

Richard J. Stillman, *Public Administration: Concepts and Cases,* 8th ed. (Boston: Houghton Mifflin, 2005), paperback.

Optional Texts

Frederick C. Mosher, *Democracy and the Public Service,* 2d ed. (New York: Oxford University Press, 1982).
Frederick C. Mosher, ed., *Basic Documents of American Public Administration: 1776–1950* (New York: Holmes and Meier, 1976).
Richard J. Stillman, ed., *Basic Documents of American Public Administration Since 1950* (New York: Holmes and Meier, 1982).

Course Description

This introductory graduate-level course provides an overview of the field and serves as a basis for further study in public administration. The course assumes no prior academic background or work in public administration. It introduces students to the concepts and practices of public administration primarily from the standpoint of the institutional framework and intellectual development of American administrative practices. Much of the course material is drawn from primary sources—basic documents of American public administration, among them legislative acts, executive orders, and major commission reports. Case material and other secondary sources also will be consulted.

Each student will be part of a team research project studying one primary document. The objectives of this project are to sharpen students' research skills and enhance individual appreciation of the depth, complexity, and dilemmas of modern administrative practice. Sharing personal work-related experiences from government and other organizations also will enhance classroom learning about the realities and practice of public administration.

Attendance and punctuality are expected in all classes. If an absence is essential, please indicate the reason for the absence (if possible, ahead of time). Each class will be devoted to discussion and analysis of the specific topics indicated for that class on the syllabus. The course will be conducted primarily as a graduate seminar, which requires that each student come to each class well prepared to participate in discussions. There also will be, however, considerable lecturing by the professor. The reading assignments will be selected mainly from the four texts listed on the first page of the syllabus, although some material for class discussions will be drawn from each student's own background and work.

Grading

The grade for the semester is based on the following criteria:

- Midterm exam: 20%
- Final exam: 30%
- Written report: 30%
- Class participation, oral report: 20%

Exams will be closed book, requiring essays or short answers—predominately essays. You will be given a choice of questions (for example, three or four out of five questions). Exams cannot be made up unless you notify the professor before the time of an exam that you cannot take the exam and you have a reasonable excuse. The emphasis of both the midterm and final exams will be on integrating course material and developing ideas and perspectives on it.

The class participation grade is based on the following:

- Participation in general class discussion (the *volume* of participation counts less than *quality* and *originality*).

- Specifically assigned oral presentations during the semester (here, also, quality, originality, and thought receive higher grades).
  Specific details about the times and nature of these presentations will be discussed more fully in class.

Written Report

A written report will be prepared by teams of two or three students during the semester on one of the public papers contained in either the Mosher or the Stillman *Basic Documents* volume. The professor will help students select their topics and develop their research. Students must select the topics and have them approved by the professor by the *second week* of class; the project is due the second to last week of the class.

The papers count as 30% of the final grade and should be between 15 and 20 pages long. They should be typed, double spaced, free of errors, with bibliography and footnotes. Late papers will be marked down one letter grade (an A paper will receive a B). Students also will report their findings from this research project orally in class at designated times. Each student's contribution to the written report must be clearly indicated in the paper.

Each paper should analyze one basic document in American public administration that has served as a building block for the field. The paper should include the following parts:

Part 1: *Introduction.* Outline the content of your report.
Part 2: *Origins.* Cover the historical, social, and political background of the particular document.
Part 3: *Prescriptions.* Indicate the values, outlooks, processes, or procedures in the document under study and why they were put forward by the authors.
Part 4: *Operation.* Show how this administrative document actually was put into practice, and describe its specific achievements or failures, as well as any new problems it created.
Part 5: *Impact.* Summarize the contributions of this document to the theory and practice of public administration.
Part 6: *Conclusion.* Summarize the key ideas in your report.

This team project is expected to be a scholarly piece of firsthand research using primary sources, field interviews, and the study of documents, hearings, and the like. A polished final report that is readable and insightful is expected from each team. The professor will assign the research teams and help students develop the project.

Required Reading and Other Assignments

1. Reading assignments listed in the syllabus are to be completed before the class session for which they are assigned, and each student must come to class well prepared to participate in discussions.
2. By the second class session, please provide a *one-page* résumé. The résumé should be carefully prepared, free of typing errors, and should contain your address and phone number. The professor's résumé is attached.
3. Again, by the second week of class you should select a basic document from either the Mosher or the Stillman text to study for your term paper. Research teams will be assigned at that time.
4. Notice that during Weeks 5 and 6, 9 and 10, and 11 and 12, short informal discussions of material drawn from students' work in an organizational setting are expected. You will be asked to prepare materials and an informal talk for class on one of the discussion topics for these weeks. Be ready by the second class to select one of the six weeks for your report.
5. The oral presentations by research teams on the documents they are studying are expected either at the end of the semester or when their document is under discussion. These *formal* oral reports should be approximately 15 minutes long and should be carefully prepared for class delivery.
6. The one-hour midterm exam (which counts as 20% of your grade) is scheduled for the sixth week of class and will cover the reading material assigned through that week.
7. The three-hour final exam (which counts as 30% of your grade) will cover all the assigned material in the course and will be given at the end of the semester at a time set by the university.

Schedule of Reading and Topical Assignments

| 1ST WEEK: | INTRODUCTION |

No reading is assigned. The first session consists of introductions and a discussion of the course and the assignments.

| 2ND WEEK: | PUBLIC ADMINISTRATION AS A FIELD OF PRACTICE AND STUDY |

Readings: Wilson, "The Study of Administration," in Stillman,
                PA, Chapter 1
                Stillman, "The Study of Public Administration in the
                United States," in Stillman, *PA*, Chapter 1
Case Study: Martin, "The Blast in Centralia No. 5," in Stillman, *PA*,
                Chapter 1

| 3RD WEEK: | THE DEVELOPMENT OF BUREAUCRACY IN AMERICA |

Readings: Weber, "Bureaucracy," in Stillman, *PA*, Chapter 2
                Mosher, *Democracy and the Public Service*, Chapters 2
                and 3
                Declaration of Independence (handout)
                U.S. Constitution (handout)
                Madison, *Federalist Paper No. 51* (handout)
Case Study: Lardner, "How Kristin Died," in Stillman, *PA*,
                Chapter 2

4TH WEEK:	POLITICS AND ADMINISTRATION: THE CENTRAL PROBLEM FOR MODERN DEMOCRACY
Readings:	Review the Woodrow Wilson essay (Chapter 1) from the second week. Heclo, "Issue Networks," in Stillman, *PA*, Chapter 14 Long, "Power and Administration," in Stillman, *PA*, Chapter 4 Mosher, *Democracy and the Public Service*, Chapter 4
Case Study:	Casamayou, "The Columbia Accident," in Stillman, *PA*, Chapter 4
5TH WEEK:	ORGANIZATIONAL, LEGAL, AND CONSTITUTIONAL FORMS OF PUBLIC ADMINISTRATION: BASIC STRUCTURAL PATTERNS OF AMERICAN PUBLIC ADMINISTRATION
Readings:	Early Executive Departments; ICC Act; General Staff, Taft Report; City Manager Plan; Brownlow Report; Government Corporation Act—in Mosher, *Basic Documents*, pp. 32–39, 61–89, and 105–149
Class Exercise:	Selected students will discuss the basic organization, arrangement, and reasons for the structure in an organization where each has worked. Students are not asked to prepare a formal talk or paper, but simply to share this information with the class.
6TH WEEK:	ORGANIZATIONAL, LEGAL, AND CONSTITUTIONAL FORMS OF PUBLIC ADMINISTRATION IN THE POSTWAR ERA: CLASSICAL, COORDINATIVE, NEOCLASSICAL, AND DECENTRALIZED STRUCTURAL PATTERNS
Readings:	Hoover Report; HEW Dept., Price Report; Kestenbaum Report; ACIR Act; Ash Report; BoB Circular A-95; Economic Opportunity Act of 1964—in Stillman, *Basic Documents*, pp. 1–71
Class Exercise:	Same as 5th week.

6TH WEEK: MIDTERM EXAMINATION

An entire class period will be devoted to the hour-long exam. The exam will be explained fully in advance.

7TH AND 8TH   ALTERNATIVE APPROACHES TO PUBLIC
WEEKS: MANAGEMENT

Readings: Lindblom, "The Science of 'Muddling Through,'" in
                         Stillman, *PA*, Chapter 8
                         Mayo, "Hawthorne and the Western Electric Company,"
                         in Stillman, *PA*, Chapter 6
                         Matland, "Synthesizing the Implementation
                         Literature," in Stillman, *PA*, Chapter 13
                         Wilson, "Bureaucracy and the Public Interest," in
                         Stillman, *PA*, Chapter 15
                         Rainey and Steinbauer, "Galloping Elephants," in
                         Stillman, *PA*, Chapter 10
                         Wise, "The Public Service Culture," in Stillman, *PA*,
                         Chapter 11
Case Study: Nagel, "The MOVE Disaster," in Stillman, *PA*,
                         Chapter 8
Class Exercise: Selected students will interview someone they view as
                         an effective public manager and report to the class the
                         reasons why he/she is considered "effective."

9TH AND 10TH   PUBLIC PERSONNEL ADMINISTRATION: THE FIVE
WEEKS: SYSTEMS OF PUBLIC PERSONNEL—THEIR
                         PROBLEMS AND PROSPECTS

Readings: Stillman, "Inside Public Bureaucracy," in Stillman, *PA*,
                         Chapter 7
                         Mosher, *Democracy and the Public Service*, Chapters
                         5–7
                         Civil Service Act of 1883, in Mosher, *Basic Documents*,
                         pp. 43–61
                         Civil Service Reform Act of 1978, in Stillman, *Basic
                         Documents*, pp. 130–162
Case Study: Sontag, "Who Brought Bernadine Healy Down?" in
                         Stillman, *PA*, Chapter 11

Class Exercise:	Selected students will bring to class a brief description of the basic personnel rules and labor-management policies for an organization where they have worked. A collective bargaining agreement may serve this purpose. No formal speech is required, but students should be prepared to summarize briefly the personnel rules or labor agreement.
11TH AND 12TH WEEKS:	PUBLIC FINANCE AND BUDGETING: THE EVOLUTION AND FORMS OF BUDGETS AND THEIR ROLES IN THE PUBLIC SECTOR
Readings:	Rubin, "The Politics of Public Budgets," in Stillman, *PA*, Chapter 12
	Budget and Accounting Act of 1921, in Mosher, *Basic Documents*, pp. 89–97
	Postwar Budget Documents, in Stillman, *Basic Documents*, pp. 165–164
Case Study:	Conant, "Wisconsin's Budget Deficit," in Stillman, *PA*, Chapter 12
Class Exercise:	Selected students will bring to class a brief description of a budget, with a discussion of recent trends and projected trends. No formally prepared speech is required, but students are expected to share ideas and information on the topic.
13TH WEEK:	STRATEGIES FOR ACHIEVING ADMINISTRATIVE ACCOUNTABILITY: CHECKS ON THE BUREAUCRACY
Readings:	Waldo, "Public Administration and Ethics," in Stillman, *PA*, Chapter 16
	Legislative Reorganization Act of 1970; War Powers Act; Freedom of Information Act; "Sunset Law"; Inspector General's Office, Proposition 13—in Stillman, *Basic Documents*, pp. 267–310
Case Study:	Montjoy and Slayton, "The Case of the Butterfly Ballot," in Stillman, *PA*, Chapter 16

14TH WEEK: STUDENT RESEARCH REPORTS AND REVIEW FOR
                   FINAL EXAMINATION

15TH WEEK: FINAL EXAMINATION

Memo 5

TO: Fellow Public Administration Teachers

FROM: RJS

SUBJECT: Guest Speakers, Field Trips, Films, Videotapes, Supplementary Readings, Internet Resources, and Teaching Public Administration Online

Every instructor has a favorite story about some classroom disaster. Mine is about a guest speaker I once invited to an introductory public administration class. I feel that it is worthwhile to let students see and hear real public administrators. It also can lead to a lively class. So, usually in the first class meeting, I encourage students to suggest people they think would be interesting speakers. Early in my teaching career, one young joker suggested a fellow, let's call him Sam, as a guest speaker. Not knowing him and just acting on the student's recommendation, I asked Sam to speak to the class. Well it turned out Sam knew very little about public administration. He had been a bartender most of his life and now thought it would be a fine idea if he ran for local county sheriff. I knew trouble was ahead when Sam arrived wearing not one, but two, 45-caliber pistols strapped to his hips. Without taking a breath, it seemed, he proceeded to regale the class for the entire period on why the county should buy six new helicopters for the sheriff's department and arm them all with machine guns. When I tried to turn his monologue around to public administration, he only insisted that armed helicopters would solve, once and for all, our local crime problem. My embarrassment was profound.

I did learn a lesson, though: Be sure to interview every guest speaker ahead of time (a phone call will do), and make sure the speaker's background and

36

planned talk relate to the material under discussion. Despite Sam, I still believe in the utility of guest speakers, but only relevant and sensible ones.

Much the same holds for field trips. Students new to the field can learn many things from a well-conducted visit to a local police department, welfare office, jail, county finance office, city council meeting, or planning facility. But field trips need to be carefully scheduled in advance, and the instructor should find out ahead of time what the tour covers. To be effective, the trip must clearly relate to the material under study.

Films and video presentations also can be useful. Like field trips, however, they call for careful scheduling as well as ample time for discussion. There are outstanding films about public administration subjects. Frederick Wiseman has made some excellent films on police, welfare offices, and mental institutions. Films that are my favorites include *Henry V*, *The Caine Mutiny*, *Lean on Me*, *Stand by Me*, and *M.A.S.H.* (for more options see the attached list of suggested films on pages 42–44 of this memo). They illustrate public administration concepts; but permission must be obtained from their copyright holders to show them in class. Also some even older films—like *Command Decision* and *Catch-22*—are relevant and well done. If your institution has videotaping facilities, you can tape students' oral reports and then replay them on video screens, asking the students to critique their presentations.

I also find handouts useful. I assign the Declaration of Independence, the Constitution, and *Federalist Papers Nos. 10* and *51* as part of the required readings for undergraduate and graduate courses. I encourage you to do likewise.

Increasingly, learning to use the Internet as a research tool is a "must" for public administration students today. The following list of web sites in Public Administration offers excellent ideas for effectively using these educational resources.[*]

Finally, online learning is growing throughout the field, but the jury is still out on its overall value as a pedagogical tool. For those interested in research on its pros and cons as a teaching method, I have included an essay by Matthew Mingus, "Toward Understanding the Culture of Internet-Mediated Learning," on pages 45–60 of this memo.

Web Sites in Public Administration

General Information

1. **http://www.fedworld.gov**
   This web site was created in order to facilitate the dissemination of information to the public and the federal government. The site provides access to a wide variety of databases, and allows the viewer to search, locate, order, and acquire a wide range of government and business information.

---

[*] As found at www.uta.edu/supa/academics/pa-links.htm.

2. **http://fic.info.gov**
   This site describes telephone service for locating federal government information, provides a list of toll-free FIC phone numbers and answers to many of the most commonly asked questions about federal services.

3. **http://thomas.loc.gov/**
   This web site provides a wealth of information on Congress and the legislative process.

Newspapers/Journals

4. **http://www.policy.com/**
   Policy.com is an online newspaper providing up-to-date information on current public policy issues.

5. **http://www.aspanet.org/publications/par/index2.html**
   The *Public Administration Review* contains articles on a diverse range of topics in the fields of public service and public sector management.

6. **http://movingideas.org/**
   This online magazine, *Moving Ideas Network*, provides links to articles discussing various public policy issues such as economic policy, politics and civil life, welfare and families, health policy, education, and old and new media. The site also provides links to a variety of online progressive journals and foundations dealing with public policy.

7. **http://www.pamij.com/**
   The home page of the online *Journal of Public Administration and Management*.

8. **http://www.govtech.net/**
   The home page for *The Government Technology Magazine*. The magazine focuses on solutions and resources available for governance in the information age.

9. **http://www.familiesusa.org/**
   Consumer voice for health care, offering articles and reports on health care, politics, reform, Medicare and Medicaid, and other health care issues for women, senior citizens, and lower-income people.

10. **http://www.library.vcu.edu/guides/pubadm.html#dict**
    This site lists a number of books, research guides, and encyclopedias on the topic of public administration.

Organizations

11. **http://aspanet.org/**
     The American Society for Public Administration is the oldest and most formidable professional association dedicated to the study of public administration. Its home page provides access to the Society's council minutes and recent papers, as well as links to the Society's current projects and other relevant web pages.

12. **http://www.napawash.org/**
     The National Academy of Public Administration is an independent, nonpartisan organization chartered by Congress to help federal, state, and local governments improve their effectiveness, efficiency, and accountability.

13. **http://www.eeoc.gov/**
     The home page of the U.S. Equal Opportunity Employment Commission.

14. **http://www.excelgov.org/**
     The Council for Excellence in Government is a national organization dedicated to improving the performance of American government.

15. **http://www.statesnews.org/**
     Nonprofit organization that seeks to foster excellence in state government. Web page includes information on the activities of regional organizations, issue alerts which inform members of breaking news that affects state government, press releases, and suggested state legislation on a variety of issues.

16. **http://andromeda.rutgers.edu/~ncpp/ncpp.html**
     The home page of the National Center for Public Productivity. The NCPP is a research and public service organization dedicated to improving productivity in the public sector. The web site focuses on the performance evaluation and best practices.

17. **http://www.urban.org/**
     The home page for the Urban Institute, a nonpartisan economic and social policy research organization. The site provides information on research concerning the nation's social and economic problems and the government policies and public and private programs designed to alleviate them.

Education

18. **http://www.hallway.org/**
    The Electronic Hallway offers teaching aids, such as role-plays, teaching exercises, teaching cases and workshops, and curriculum planning resources for faculty focusing on public administration and public policy. The Electronic Hallway is also developing collections on nonprofit management, social work, political science, and health administration.

19. **http://civnet.org/**
    Civnet is a web site for civic education practitioners (teachers, teacher trainers, curriculum designers) as well as scholars, policymakers, civic-minded journalists, and nongovernmental organizations (NGOs) promoting civil society all over the world.

20. **http://deming.ces.clemson.edu/pub/psci/**
    The Public Sector Continuous Improvement Site aims to help public sector employees improve their organizations. The site provides access to a library of related materials such as articles, case studies, files, and more.

Government Agencies

21. **http://www.dol.gov/**
    The home page of the Department of Labor.

22. **http://www.usdoj.gov/**
    The Department of Justice home page.

23. **http://www.ed.gov/**
    The home page for the Department of Education.

24. **http://www.hhs.gov/**
    The home page for the Department of Health and Human Services.

25. **http://hud.gov/**
    The home page for the Department of Housing and Urban Development.

26. **http://www.treas.gov/**
    The home page for the Treasury Department.

27. **http://www.state.gov/**
    The home page for the Department of State.

28. **http://www.fda.gov/**
    The home page for the Food and Drug Administration.

29. **http://www.defenselink.mil/**
    The home page for the Department of Defense.

30. **http://www.commerce.gov/**
    The home page for the Department of Commerce.

Other Sites

31. **http://www.arnet.gov/index.html**
    The home page for the Acquisition Reform Network provides information on how the government obtains goods and services. It links to its reference corner, acquisition opportunities, acquisition best practices, and training information.

32. **http://www.afscme.org/**
    The home page for the nation's largest public employee and health care workers union.

33. **http://www.narc.org/**
    This site contains information about agencies engaged in comprehensive regional planning and coordination. The sponsors promote cooperation among state and local governments and among public, private, and civic organizations at the regional level.

34. **http://www.stateline.org/**
    Operated by the Pew Center on the States, this site's goal is to help journalists, policymakers, and engaged citizens become better informed about innovative public policies.

Some Films About Public Administration and Policymaking

In Teaching

Au Revoir Les Enfants
The Beautiful Blond from Bashful
  Bend
Dead Poets Society
Lean on Me
Mr. Holland's Opus
Stand and Deliver

In Politics

Abe Lincoln in Illinois
Advise and Consent
All the King's Men
The Best Man
City Hall
The Contender
JFK
Mr. Smith Goes to Washington
Nixon
Primary Colors
The Seduction of Joe Tynan
Sunrise at Campobello
Thirteen Days
The War Room

In Science Fiction

The Andromeda Syndrome
Blade Runner
Contact
The Disk
Dune
Excalibur
Fahrenheit 451
1984
Planet of the Apes
Space Odyssey 2001

Star Wars
THX

In Sports

The Babe
Bull Durham
Breaking Away
Cool Running
The Gladiator
Hoop Dreams
Hoosiers
Jackie Robinson Story
Jerry Maguire
White Squall

About Women

Angela's Ashes
Cleopatra
Dead Man Walking
Elizabeth
Erin Brokovich
Fried Green Tomatoes
Gorillas in the Mist
A League of Their Own
Lilies in the Field
Marie
The Messenger
My Cousin Vinny
Norma Rae
Places in the Heart
Prime Suspect
Silkwood
Sophie's Choice

In Business

Bugsy
Cheaper by the Dozen
Citizen Kane
Efficiency Expert
The Insider
The Man in the Grey Flannel Suit
The Man in the White Suit
Roger and Me
Tucker
Wall Street

In Courts, Prisons, and Policing

And Justice for All
The Border
Brubaker
The Caine Mutiny
A Civil Action
Die Hard
A Few Good Men
Hoffa
In the Heat of the Night
In the Name of the Father
The Onion Field
Shawshank Redemption
Twelve Angry Men
The Verdict

In the Media

Bulworth
A Face in the Crowd
My Girl Friday
Network
News at Eleven
The Player
Wag the Dog

About Minorities

American Me
And the Band Played On
Braveheart
The Burning Season
Colors
Cry the Beloved Country
Divided We Fall
General Dell Rovere
Gentlemen's Agreement
Harvest of Shame
It's a Beautiful Life
Jacob the Liar
Man for All Seasons
The Milagro Beanfield War
Miss Evers' Boys
Philadelphia
Roots
Viva Zapata

In Westerns

The Cheyenne Social Club
Dances with Wolves
High Noon
The Ox Bow Incident
The Shootist
Stage Coach

In War

All Quiet on the Western Front
Battle of the Bulge
Breaker Morant
The Bridge
Bridge Over the River Kwai
A Bridge Too Far
Casualties of War
Command Decision
Courage Under Fire
Crimson Tide
Das Boot

Enemies at the Gate
A Few Good Men
From Here to Eternity
Gallipoli
Gettysburg
Glory
The Grand Illusion
Hitler
Hunt for Red October
Mutiny on the Bounty
Napoleon
Patriot Games
Patton
Platoon
Run Silent, Run Deep
Saving Private Ryan
Schindler's List
Twelve O'Clock High
Under Fire

In Spy Stories

Casablanca
Clear and Present Danger
The Man Who Knew Too Much
Notorious
The Spy that Came in from the Cold
The 39 Steps
The Ugly American

From Great Stories

American Beauty
The Bicycle Thief
Billy Budd
Bob Roberts

Elmer Gantry
Forrest Gump
Gone with the Wind
The Great Santini
Henry V (1989 version)
Ikiru
It's a Wonderful Life
Kagemusha
King David
King Lear
Les Miserables
Lion King
Lord Jim
Lord of the Flies
Moby Dick
One Flew Over the Cuckoo's Nest
The Overcoat
The Plague
RAN
Richard III (1995 version)
Romero
Shogun
Sound of Music
The Three Musketeers
Watership Down
Wild River

In Docu-dramas

Fire and Rain
Gandhi
Hiroshima
Judgment at Nuremburg
Laurence of Arabia
The Sorrow and the Pity
Stonewall
Triumph of the Will

Toward Understanding the Culture of Internet-Mediated Learning

Matthew S. Mingus
Western Michigan University[*]

Abstract

Peterson's college guide reported in 1997 that 762 educational institutions were offering courses via the internet, more than a 700 percent increase since 1994. In spite of this trend, little research on the learning culture of these internet-mediated courses exists. This paper reports on an ethnographic study of the CU Online program at the University of Colorado at Denver and explores five themes that emerge for the research agenda for the online learning culture: the importance of human interaction, the student work ethic, personal characteristics, the thoughtfulness of student comments in an asynchronous environment, and the instructor's critical role as moderator of the learning process. The primary agenda items are intended to help instructors make the difficult choice of whether to use asynchronous or real-time communication in their course designs and to explore ways to support healthy group dynamics in the electronic frontier.[1]

The American educational system continually adapts to changes in resources, society, and demographics, and is now faced with many decisions related to the pervasive influence of technology. While technological possibilities are rapidly transforming today's educational system, little research exists on how these changes affect the learning culture at the college level. This article reports on research intended to explore the culture of the online course.

"Culture" is used in its familiar sense to denote the habits, customs, and patterns of human interactions in a specific setting. The research approach is ethnographic in the sense in which Catherine Marshall and Gretchen B. Rossman (1995, 81) use the term when they state that "ethnographic interviewing elicits the cognitive structures guiding participants' worldviews." This article derives themes for further research on the learning culture of Internet-mediated education by asking "What learning culture develops as students interact with one

---

[*] Matthew S. Mingus is an assistant professor in the School of Public Affairs and Administration at Western Michigan University. His primary research interests include comparative network theory, U.S.-Canadian relations, and speculative/futuristic topics such as quantum administration. He teaches MPA courses including foundations of public administration, organizational theory, and research methods. Mingus earned his Ph.D. in public administration from the University of Colorado at Denver. Reprinted by permission from Matthew S. Mingus, "Toward Understanding the Culture of Internet-Mediated Learning," from *Journal of Public Affairs Education*, 5 (1999).

Reprinted by permission from Matthew S. Mingus, "Toward Understanding the Culture of Internet-Mediated Learning," from *Journal of Public Affairs Education*, 5 (1999).

another and the instructor primarily in writing and primarily in asynchronous[2] time?"

CU Online, Growth, and the Internet Culture

The University of Colorado "CU Online" program delivers more than one hundred courses from across the disciplinary spectrum, and students regularly take courses without meeting the professor or other students in a face-to-face setting. MPA core courses at the Graduate School of Public Affairs (GSPA) are available for credit in an on-line format, meaning that students interact with each other and the instructor via electronic mail and computer conferencing—posting comments to the course home page, using a listserv to email a group rather than one individual, and occasionally communicating in real-time chat rooms.

The development of this online program, according to Linda deLeon, former MPA director at GSPA, is based in large part on the belief that educational institutions must actively reach out to potential markets. This belief has also led GSPA into evening courses, a distant education program based in Grand Junction, Colorado, and courses that take place on two or three intensive weekends. Rather than being alone in this web-based educational environment, more than one million students are "plugged into the virtual college classroom" and 762 schools used the Internet to deliver courses in 1997, up from just 93 in 1994 (Gubernick and Ebeling, 1997, 84–85). As of April 1999, the Maricopa Center for Learning and Instruction web site provided more than 711 examples of how the web is used as a medium for learning (http://www.mcli.dist.maricopa.edu/tl/about.html).

It is especially important to examine the impact of these trends on the learning culture. Culture is intimately connected with the concept of community. One writer refers to the information superhighway, a popular term for the Internet and the World Wide Web, as "a road to misery" (Krautz, 1996, 22), and others assert its ability to destroy basic civil liberties, to make our society less literate, and even to reduce our ability to speak in complete sentences (Tough, 1995). Nevertheless, its advantages are touted far more frequently, including its uses in virtual surgery and virtual design for medical and architectural education (Briggs, 1996) and in the production of "just in time" training programs—intensive, skills-oriented courses delivered when the workforce needs the skill rather than as part of some potentially long-forgotten degree program—at a realistic price (Phillips, 1998). Its advantages also include increasing the focus on social capital rather than marketplace values (Rifkin, 1996) and increasing our willingness to explore new relationships and even new identities (Turkle, 1995). A key figure in the communitarian movement, Amitai Etzioni, highlights the benefits of online communities to allow those who cannot leave home or are otherwise relatively isolated to participate in society, to allow communities to form across national boundaries and geographical barriers, and to maintain a better memory than the time-worn "town meeting" approach (Etzioni and Etzioni, 1997).

The culture of the Internet—versus the impact of the Internet on our culture—has also been the source of much writing. Five similarities emerge from recent literature on this culture (Heim, 1993; Kiesler, 1997; Drucker, 1998). First, Internet-mediated communication or some similar technology is here to stay (also see McC. Adams, 1997) and is being embraced by thousands of new individuals each passing day. Secondly, the proliferation of interactive, multi-participant games and nonerotic chat groups provides ample evidence that people quickly learn "affect" and feelings without requiring a face-to-face setting (also see Morningstar and Farmer, 1991). An implication of this is that the pre-1960s "neighborhood as community" is receding into history as communities are increasingly based on common interests and common problems rather than geographic proximity. Third, the concentration of leadership and power may change dramatically as the Internet continues to increase the efficiency of participation. Fourth, people can be smart buyers and smart users of information, but they must first have a healthy education because the Internet, at its best, assumes one knows what to look for. Finally, the hypertext and multimedia aspects of the Internet force us to start asking challenging ontological questions such as "What is the boundary between fact and fiction?" and "What is life?" (see also Benedikt, 1991; Turkle, 1995).

Society and culture are indeed changing because of the pervasive influence of the Internet and related technologies. Although the future is far from certain, it is clear that these online communities are part of the new mix of relationships that will help to sustain us as individuals. This environment forms the setting for this ethnographic study on the learning culture of Internet-mediated courses.

Methodology

As an exploratory study, this research seeks to identify themes that arise in an online learning environment. The ethnographic focus is intended to discover more about students' experiences rather than to generalize to the student population at the University of Colorado or elsewhere. As such, three processes were used to obtain information for this project: (1) in-depth interviews with six students, three each from two different online courses; (2) informal discussions with six professors in person and via the telephone; and (3) an examination of the web sites for three different online courses.

I selected an "active interviewing" approach because I believe that interviews are more than an extraction of data from informants and because I anticipated that the experience levels of the informants with various types of technology would vary widely. Active interviewing assumes that interviewer objectivity is a myth and that, knowingly or otherwise, everything the interviewer does helps to shape the responses of the informants (Holstein and Gubrium, 1995). The interviewer offers informants "pertinent ways of conceptualizing issues and making connections" and researchers can "recognize how the interviewers shaped these conversations without rejecting the final products as somehow defiled or tainted" (39, 50).

I sought to have each informant think about the two course formats—i.e., the traditional classroom course and the Internet-mediated course—from a number of different perspectives—e.g., their own perspective, the perspective of a student in the classroom-based course, and the instructor's perspective. Active interviewing presumes that people are always responding from specific points of view and that they are quite capable of examining issues from multiple perspectives (Holstein and Gubrium, 1995).

Students were selected at random from the course lists for Democracy and Policy Making, an MPA core course, and Race and Ethnicity, an undergraduate sociology course that fulfills a multicultural education requirement. I expected that together these courses would attract students from the full range of the student body in each of the two programs. In actuality, each of the undergraduate students was taking three online courses and one of the graduate students was also taking online courses at Regis University in Denver. In this way, the informant's experience turned out to be far broader than anticipated. I personally conducted the interviews in all cases and allowed the informants to select the location and timing of the meeting.

In addition to the student interviews that serve as the main data for this research, 10- to 20-minute conversations with six professors—three of whom had online teaching experience—helped provide perspective for this study. These instructors taught a range of courses from undergraduate English, sociology, and mathematics to graduate courses in public policy, qualitative analysis, and public management. Two had one or two years of teaching experience and four were veterans with ten or more years of experience. The three with online teaching experience were selected because they taught courses the student informants were taking, and the other three were selected from instructors I knew (including one known to still use the pencil and paper method for everything).

An examination of three course web sites gave me general background information on the environment before I interviewed the informants, akin to participant observation, and was used after the interviews to confirm several student ideas during the analysis of the interview transcripts.

Profile of Informants

The three MPA students are called Marilyn, Sandra, and Hector. Marilyn has a background in social work and psychology and is focusing on developing her skills in nonprofit management. She is in her mid-40s with a husband and two children. Sandra works 60-hour weeks in a service-sector business, has an infant daughter and has never been married, and seems uncertain why she is working on an MPA except that she is interested in electoral politics as a future career option. Hector works for a public sector consulting firm, had only a passing familiarity with the Internet prior to taking his first online course, and is motivated to take online courses to avoid having evening classes cut into family time.

The three undergraduate students are called Maria, Lisa, and Bob. Maria switched to taking a full load of online courses in her senior year when she gave birth to her second child. Financially and personally, it is extremely helpful to Maria to be the primary caregiver for her children. Lisa is a traditional college student who lives at home with her parents, works full time to afford her education, and turned to CU Online to eliminate a 30-minute commute to campus. Bob is an older undergraduate student who is receiving disability payments that allow him to focus on school. He has a hand and foot disability that makes travel to campus difficult and he displayed an exceptional understanding of the technology of the Internet and web-based instruction.

An ethnographic study seeks to learn from the experience of informants rather than to develop generalizable conclusions, so a diversity of backgrounds is critical because it increases the range of experience among informants. Each informant completed a demographic form at the conclusion of the interview. Demographic responses demonstrated that the informants represented a diverse spectrum in terms of employment status, course loads, family size and marital status, ethnicity, and age. All had access to computers at home and half of them used computers at work for course-related purposes. Only one student lived more than 20 miles from campus and one person had a disability that made getting to campus difficult. The demographic profiles confirmed that a rather broad group of informants resulted from the random selection process.

Findings: Five Themes from the Virtual Classroom

A rich body of literature is developing around the "virtual classroom" (Hiltz, 1994; Tiffin and Rajasingham, 1995; Wells, 1992) and some research focuses on the culture of distance learning (Evans, 1994; Freddolino, 1996). Five themes that emerged from this research project can guide the design of future research on the learning culture of Internet-mediated courses. A summary of the key findings is presented at the end of this [memo]. These findings present a basis for designing future cross-site research by helping to ensure that surveys or other instruments are well grounded in the student experience.

Theme 1: Importance of Interaction

Human interaction includes student-student, student-teacher, and small group interaction. Relationships are expected to be critical in the online environment, just as Paul Freddolino (1996) has confirmed that they are critical in interactive television classrooms. Informants' comments suggest that small group interaction may be weakened in the online setting, but student-teacher interaction appears to be strengthened. The good news is that, like most distance education models, Internet-mediated instruction can actually facilitate the ongoing transition from the one-way-transmission-of-information model to the emergent learner paradigm that stresses faculty-student and student-student collaboration (McLellan, 1998; Sullivan, 1997, 35; Wilson and Ryder, 1996).

The record on the "loss of classroom interaction" myth expressed by the faculty members who had not taught online courses is mixed. Marilyn said, "I think that there are probably a lot of ideas that are kicked around in the classroom that I'm missing taking a lot of online classes." While she consistently expressed this view and explained well why she still decided to take numerous online courses, she also expressed the view that professors should structure class so that student comments go to all students via computer conferencing, rather than just being sent to the professor. In her mind, classes where this was done had far more student-student interaction.

This same idea was reflected among several other informants who felt that the belief that human interaction is "lost" is predicated upon the assumption of an "ideal" classroom where meaningful interaction is taking place. These students had little experience in such an ideal classroom. David A. Karp and William C. Yoels (1976) questioned the existence of this ideal classroom in their classic study of the classroom culture. Their study observed an array of undergraduate courses and noted that "in classes with less than 40 students, between 4 and 5 students account for 75 percent of the total interactions per session; in classes of more than 40 students, between 2 and 3 students account for 51 percent of the total interactions per session" (Karp and Yoels, 1976, 423).

In *Teaching Sociology*, Kim M. King (1994, 174) reiterates this point: "Despite the positive aspects of classroom discussion, many of us know that it does not always work. In many situations, classroom discussions leave much to be desired." Hope exists for worthwhile computer-based classroom discussions because, as King stresses, she used Vax Notes on a mainframe computer to allow students to keep class journals. After a term using this computer-mediated conferencing system, King (1994, 175) realized "that in fact we were holding classroom discussions—thought-provoking, peer-oriented discussions—outside the classroom." Hilary McLellan's (1998) recent research also supports this notion that computer conferencing generates dynamic interaction.

Nevertheless, it is conceivable that students who do not generally participate in class discussions still learn from these discussions; this might explain why each of the informants expressed at least a mild sentiment that the online courses were missing something in the way of student-student interaction. In most cases, they thought that the instructor could minimize this loss through more active use of computer conferencing tools to create classroom-like discussions and by stepping in to remind students of the importance of such discussion tools.

Moving to the topic of student-professor interaction, Lisa made this comment in response to a quite general question on the difference between the online and classroom formats:

> I like the fact that the instructor is more accessible through an online course than in a traditional classroom. He stands up there and he lectures for 45 minutes to an hour and then that's it. I feel more uncomfortable going up to them and meeting them during their office hours, which don't correlate with my schedule. [Now] I can email my professor, he can email me back, and we can have a discussion. I like that much better than in a traditional classroom.

Between the telephone and email, five of the six informants expressed solid contact with their instructors. Previous research on distance education also revealed no significant affective differences in the student-teacher interaction of in-class and distance education students, but this was in an environment in which classes met at remote locations and the teacher was "present" in real-time video (Thomerson and Smith, 1996).

The third area of this human interaction theme concerns the use of small groups. Suffice it to say that none of the six students reported positive small group experiences in online classes, although all three of the course web sites that were examined had some form of small group discussions or projects built into the course structure. Based on the comments, there appears to be a psychological distance created through electronic communications that enabled many students to ignore even the urgent need to work together to get a project completed by a deadline. Michael Heim (1991, 75–76) predicted similar results as the disembodied community of the Internet expanded.

This is an area deserving of more study as online programs seek improvement, especially because small groups are increasingly used in education to increase meaningful student interaction. Overall, small group interaction was the area in which human interaction appeared compromised in this learning culture, although the web site review suggested that the particular courses being studied lacked techniques to establish individual responsibility for group participation.

Theme 2: Student Work Ethic

The professors and the students in this study believed that students in the online format worked harder on their reading and kept more up to date on their assignments than students in the classroom setting. Two potential causes were identified: (1) increased instructor expectations, and (2) self-selection of good readers into the online course format.

Maria expressed a common view of instructor expectations:

Q: Do you feel the education level that you're getting is about the same as in the classroom?

A: One of the professors I'm taking is in my department and I've taken him in the classroom before, and I tend to notice that he works us harder online than he did in class. Which would be totally opposite from what I'm thinking, you know. You would think that he would do exactly the same as he's doing in class . . . [yet] online he has questions due weekly. I mean we're not talking about just paragraph questions. He's making us write papers on them.

This is similar to comments from other students in that the instructor's requirements and expectations were driving the additional workload. In general, students were required to submit a two- or three-page paper in place of what might ordinarily be termed "classroom participation." Therefore, this research left little doubt that each student must stay up to date because they are not able to rely on a minority of class members to pull the weight in classroom discussion.

On top of this, these students identified themselves as readers. Some form of thoughtful, self-selecting behavior may be at play as students decide whether or not to register for online courses. Even the two informants who were extremely social and missed the classroom interaction expressed the view that they learn well by reading. They commented, for example, "I get very bored [in class]. My mind's going a hundred miles an hour thinking of other things I could be doing. I'd rather just be able to read the books, do the work, and hand it in." Another student stated, "The reason I took this course online is because the other way [in a different class with the same instructor] I didn't go to class because it didn't hold my attention. I could read it in the book."

Lisa summed up the overall time commitment by stating that she could generally do her schoolwork—reading assignments, computer conferencing, and online tests and quizzes—from 10 A.M. to 1 P.M. each day before she went to work. For nine semester hours, she put in fifteen hours of effort per week, equivalent to what she would previously have committed to class time plus an additional two hours per class per week. This time commitment is a bit light compared to the undergraduate professor's rule of thumb of spending three hours outside class each week, on average, for a three-credit-hour class. Student productivity during these hours, however, was reportedly extremely high. This means that "time commitment" and "perceived workload" may not be comparable concepts, and both are worthy targets for future research.

Working harder is not necessarily an integral part of the online learning culture. Student perceptions of a heavy workload may derive from instructors' responses as they venture into unfamiliar territory and increase written assignments to help ensure that students learn. It may also be that instructors have a heightened awareness of the need to secure credibility for online courses. Likewise, the issue of good readers self-selecting into—or poor readers self-selecting out of—the online format is worthy of additional study.

Theme 3: Personal Characteristics

The online format may be less biased toward particular personalities than the classroom setting because it can remove the face-to-face and real-time dynamics of the classroom culture. There is evidence that the more vocal and visible students in the traditional classroom earn better grades (Karp and Yoels, 1976). The third theme here suggests that personality biases may be reduced in the online setting so that the more extroverted student is not perceived almost reflexively as the better student simply because the more introverted student is too quiet to label. Hector, a student with a wealth of training and experience in multiculturalism, described this clearly: "It might be personality. It might be a cultural issue. I don't know, but for whatever reason you can identify some students who just don't want to participate in open discussions. Online there's no way you can tell."

Genie Stowers (1995) confirmed this "participation dynamic" as she found that computer conferencing appears to equalize men's and women's involvement in discussions. The informants expressed a number of other ways in which the online setting helped them with personality issues that would have been a concern in the classroom. The idea of equalizing introverts and extroverts is too limiting and stereotypical to describe this issue; however, the concept that many personal factors keep students from speaking up in class and that they are more likely to "speak up" in the online setting is an accurate depiction. Sandra got to the heart of the personality issue in describing herself:

Q: Are you someone, then, who generally would ask questions in class in a normal classroom setting?

A: No. Well if something hits me right, you know, but no. I'm a thinker. I'm a writer, you know. Sometimes I don't even listen in the classroom. Sometimes I've got 15 million other things on my mind about my day, and that makes it hard. Because then you're not getting—I'm not getting—what I need to get out of my education because I'm not in the mood for it or whatever.

"Introverted" does not describe Sandra's style in the least. Yet she is clearly one of the majority of students that are seldom heard from in the classroom setting (Karp and Yoels, 1976). Personality traits that make her a quiet student in class worked less to her disadvantage in the online course because she came to class when she was ready. The same is true of Maria, although she has a very different personality. Maria explained that she fails to understand what many students are thinking in class because the interaction is limited, while at the same time expressing her own fear of saying things in class because she does not have adequate time to think through her thoughts. These are not uncommon concerns, and they point to another personal characteristic that lead students to benefit from the online setting: asynchronous communication allows them ample time to think.

Finally, another person who may be more comfortable in the online environment is the person who feels negative reactions or discrimination from others because of his or her appearance. For example, a significantly overweight informant expressed doubt about her own appearance a number of times during the interview. She felt she was developing an online friend and stated, "I feel like I'm almost getting to know him through this, even though I've never met him. I have no idea what he looks like. I like that. I really enjoy that because it's like there's no preconceived notion of somebody just because you meet them first. You're going to know them through their words and that's usually the most important part of a person."

The more anonymous nature of the online setting, at least in the context of a primarily text-based, online structure, thus helps protect against the fear that one's weight, race, or general appearance may inhibit the development of interaction. It seems reasonable that if students have this concern when interacting with classmates, as indicated by several of the informants, then they may also fear a similar bias on the part of the classroom instructor.

Theme 4: Thoughtful Comments in an Asynchronous Environment

The use of email and computer conferencing as the primary means of communication in the course web sites reviewed for this study appeared to produce higher-quality student comments and perhaps reduced student inhibitions about speaking up in class. This theme has appealing surface validity because the asynchronous and somewhat anonymous nature of the text-based, online course format provides more time for students to think and check their facts prior to making comments and may reduce the need to be accepted by fellow students because of the physical distance between them.

Maria, for example, expressed concern about "saying something stupid" in class and pointed out that the online format frees her to think more before making comments. Lisa supported this with additional detail when speaking of her Race and Ethnicity course:

Q: So the email is less spontaneous and in that class this helps?

A: Yes, that helps a lot. I mean the conversations are more to the point and more "Let's not beat around the bush," and also "I disagree with you but let me tell you why," and it's structured.

Sandra provided a more representative comment on this topic: "I think it allows for more thoughtful answers. Because you read the email, you look at it. You may log off and you may think about it and then you may just be lying there in bed in the middle of the night and think of something important, and you log on and you say it. You don't have that opportunity [to think] in the classroom."

The informants and several of the professors with online teaching experience consistently expressed that communications in the online format were better thought out by the students. There was inconsistency about whether the format fostered more critical or confrontational communications. Some students clearly retained a concern for being socially accepted by their classmates in the online setting. While one might assume that "more thought out" is a positive attribute, Hector made it clear that a potential downside is the loss of classroom spontaneity: "I miss having the experience of sharing and listening and learning from other students as well as from the professor . . . and being able to respond to questions immediately and having . . . impromptu discussions versus the online. It's very structured and you have time to think about how it is that you want to respond."

Theme 5: Critical Role of the Instructor as Moderator

Technology limitations or innovations are less critical than the role of the instructor on student attitudes about the online learning culture—i.e., that technology is a tool rather than a "solution" to weaknesses in the educational system. In brief, this forms the fifth theme, which is that the instructor makes a tremendous difference in the success of the online course rather than the limitations or innovations of the technology. Instructors who use this tool wisely will best promote student learning.

An overwhelming portion of student comments confirm this critical role of the instructor, less as lecturer and purveyor of knowledge than as moderator or facilitator of the learning process. Interestingly enough, this is in keeping with the suggested role of the instructor to best facilitate learning for women (Lundeberg and Moch, 1995) and with a constructivist educational approach, which has been specifically researched in relation to computer-mediated distance education. David Jonassen and others (1995, 8) describe constructivist learning in the following manner: "Students and instructors can build meaning, understanding, and relevant practice together and go far beyond the mere movement of information from instructors' minds to students' notebooks." They state that the fundamental principle is "systematically alternating control between teacher and students" and that this pedagogy may easily be adapted to the online environment, in which, research indicates, the instructors' contribution to the verbal exchange drops from about 80 percent in the average classroom to roughly 10 to 15 percent in the online environment (Jonassen et al., 1995, 16).

Informant comments as well as the review of discussion groups in the course web sites confirmed this research, yet students made detailed comments about the role of the instructor, including comments supporting the following ideas:

- It is critical to be able to reach the instructor by telephone or in person because sometimes email is just not satisfactory.

- The instructor frequently receives messages from the students and determines which messages to send to the entire class.

- If the instructor is active in threaded discussions, "you . . . have a little bit of a lecture and a classroom setting going on" via the web site.

- Instructors who fail to respond to email or to provide feedback on assignments in a timely fashion create unnecessary student anxiety.

- The instructor must monitor small group interaction and prod groups along when they are lagging.

These ideas support the notion that instructors must shift their mindset from that of a lecturer to that of a moderator (many instructors have already made this shift in the classroom) and they support the notion that the instructor, rather than the technology, drives the success of the course.

Concluding Comments

Technology "has tended to prove unique among human cultural achievements in being cumulative and irreversible. Moreover, its improvement through time has not been constant or continuous but instead has taken the form of an irregular series of powerful thrusts or waves" (McC. Adams, 1997, 950).

As Robert McC. Adams notes, technological developments generally burst upon the scene and seldom simply disappear. Internet-mediated education has been made possible because of a burst of technology that continues and is becoming increasingly popular because it is convenient and efficient from the perspective of the consumer—the student. Many informants felt more connected to instructors than in the classroom setting, and one felt she had developed a friend who was in several of her online classes, so it is clear that the online learning culture is a culture rather than a bunch of disassociated individuals.

This research suggests avenues for further study of the learning culture that is developing in Internet-mediated courses. Although the findings are best summarized in the summary at the end of this [memo], two points are worthy of elaboration. First, online technology is advancing to the point where online courses can take place in a real-time environment with audio and video links. Instructors will be increasingly forced to decide whether to replicate the real-time dynamics of the classroom or to exercise the advantages of asynchronous communication. The types of learners who have the most to gain from online courses may need the asynchronous environment and the anonymous nature of a text-based environment. Providing additional information to help instructors make this decision is perhaps the primary item on the research agenda, because their decisions may have profound implications for the learning culture that develops.

Second, online rules of participation may need to be developed and enforced in order to increase the value of group discussions and assignments. Research into this area, especially the study of Internet-mediated courses that can provide evidence of effective group dynamics, is suggested by this exploration of the learning culture. Face-to-face interaction is scripted by years of socialization, and the learning culture for Internet-mediated courses may need support to ensure that the culture develops in a productive manner. Issues such as rudeness and avoidance of group commitments can be monitored and addressed in this environment, and this research suggests that supportive measures in this area need to be studied.

Notes

1. I thank Linda deLeon, associate professor at the University of Colorado at Denver's Graduate School of Public Affairs, for her assistance in conceptualizing this material. I also appreciate the improvements to the quality and clarity of this article made by the symposium editor and anonymous reviewers.
2. *Asynchronous communication* means the receiver of a message is not listening to or reading the message at the same time that the sender is speaking or writing the message. Internet users often call this *virtual time.* In contrast, *real time* is used in this article to denote the sender and receiver of a message interacting at the same point in time.

References

Benedikt, Michael. 1991. "Introduction." In *Cyberspace: First Steps,* Michael Benedikt, ed. Cambridge, MA: MIT Press, 1–25.

Briggs, John C. 1996. "The Promise of Virtual Reality." *The Futurist,* 30(5): 13–18.

Drucker Foundation. 1998. *The Community of the Future.* Frances Hesselbein, Marshall Goldsmith, Richard Beckhard, and Richard F. Schubert, eds. San Francisco: Jossey-Bass Publishers.

Etzioni, Amitai and Oren Etzioni. 1997. "Communities: Virtual vs. Real." *Science,* 277(5324): 295.

Evans, Terry. 1994. *Understanding Learners in Open and Distance Education.* London: Kogan Page.

Freddolino, Paul P. 1996. "The Importance of Relationships for a Quality Learning Environment in Interactive TV Classrooms." *Journal of Education for Business,* 71(4): 205–209.

Gubernick, Lisa and Ashlea Ebeling. 1997. "I got my degree through E-mail." *Forbes,* 159(12): 84–92.

Heim, Michael. 1993. *The Metaphysics of Virtual Reality.* New York: Oxford University Press.

Heim, Michael. 1991. "The Erotic Ontology of Cyberspace." In *Cyberspace: First Steps.* Michael Benedikt, ed. Cambridge, MA: MIT Press, 59–80.

Hiltz, Starr Roxanne. 1994. *The Virtual Classroom: Learning Without Limits via Computer Networks.* Norwood, NJ: Ablex.

Holstein, James A. and Jaber F. Gubrium. 1995. *The Active Interview: Qualitative Research Methods Series.* Thousand Oaks, CA: Sage Publications.

Jonassen, David, Mark Davison, Mauri Collins, John Campbell, and Brenda Bannan Haag. 1995. "Constructivism and Computer-Mediated Communication in Distance Education." *American Journal of Distance Education,* 9(2): 7–26.

Karp, David A. and William C. Yoels. 1976. "The College Classroom: Some Observations on the Meanings of Student Participation." *Sociology and Social Research,* 60(4): 421–439.

Kiesler, Sara, ed. 1997. *Culture of the Internet.* Mahwah, NJ: Lawrence Erlbaum Associates Publishers.

King, Kim M. 1994. "Leading Classroom Discussions: Using Computers for a New Approach." *Teaching Sociology,* 22(April): 174–182.

Krautz, Joachim. 1996. "The Information Superhighway: A Road to Misery?" *Contemporary Review,* 268(1560): 22–27.

Lundeberg, Mary Anna and Susan Diemert Moch. 1995. "Influence of Social Interaction on Cognition: Connected Learning in Science." *Journal of Higher Education,* 66(3): 312–335.

Marshall, Catherine and Gretchen B. Rossman. 1995. *Designing Qualitative Research.* Thousand Oaks, CA: Sage Publications.

McC. Adams, Robert. 1997. "Social Contexts of Technology." *Social Research,* 64(3): 947–964.

McLellan, Hilary. 1998. "The Internet as a Virtual Learning Community." *Journal of Computing in Higher Education,* 9(2): 92–112.

Morningstar, Chip and F. Randall Farmer. 1991. "The Lessons of Lucasfilm's Habitat." In *Cyberspace: First Steps,* Michael Benedikt, ed. Cambridge, MA: MIT Press, 273–301.

Phillips, Vicky. 1998. "Virtual Classrooms, Real Education." *Nation's Business,* 86(5): 41–45.

Rifkin, Jeremy. 1996. "Civil Society in the Information Age: Workerless Factories and Virtual Companies." *The Nation,* 262(8): 11–16.

Stowers, Genie N. L. 1995. "Getting Left Behind? Gender Differences in Computer Conferencing." *Public Productivity and Management Review,* 19(2): 143–159.

Sullivan, Eugene. 1997. "Campus Technology Trends." *Educational Record,* 78(1): 35–36.

Thomerson, J. D. and Clifton L. Smith. 1996. "Student Perceptions of the Affective Experiences Encountered in Distance Learning Courses." *American Journal of Distance Education,* 10(3): 37–47.

Tiffin, John and Lalita Rajasingham. 1995. *In Search of the Virtual Class. Education in an Information Society.* London: Routledge.

Tough, Paul, ed. 1995. "Forum: What Are We Doing Online?" *Harper's Magazine,* 291(1743): 35–46.

Turkle, Sherry. 1995. *Life on the Screen: Identity in the Age of the Internet.* New York: Simon and Schuster.

Wells, Rosalie. 1992. *Computer-Mediated Communication for Distance Education: An International Review of Design, Teaching, and Institutional Issues.* University Park, PA: American Center for the Study of Distance Education.

Wilson, Brent and Martin Ryder. 1996. "Dynamic Learning Communities: an Alternative to Designed Instructional Systems." *Proceedings of Selected Research and Development Presentations, 1996 National Convention of the Association for Educational Communications and Technology.* Indianapolis, IN.

Summary of Key Findings

Themes	Key Findings to Be Explored through Further Research
Importance of Interaction	Most students missed the classroom interaction, yet they felt that interaction can occur in the online setting. Student-teacher interaction was perceived as strong. Teachers likened this to individual tutorials. Small group interaction left the most to be desired (this could be the result of a self-selection bias for online students).
Student Work Ethic	Students believed they worked harder in online courses, especially on their reading assignments, and were self-defined as "readers." Instructors confirmed this perception. Students were working harder (but not necessarily investing more time) because instructors raised their expectations. For example, skipping the reading was not an option when the instructor required students to submit brief papers on the readings each week "in lieu of" class time.
Personal Characteristics	The education literature suggests extroverts are perceived as more successful in the classroom. Much more than extroversion appeared to be at play in the classroom interaction "game." Online setting provided a comfortable learning space for some people—thinkers, writers, those who are concerned about their appearance or are anxious about making "dumb" comments. Students participated in "class" when they were ready to learn.
Thoughtful Comments in Asynchronous Environment	Near universal belief among students and instructors that student comments were better thought out in the asynchronous environment. Mixed evidence on whether these comments were more forthright or confrontational. For example, one student felt class comments were very personal while another in the same class thought the comments were just politically correct.

Themes	Key Findings to Be Explored through Further Research
Critical Role of the Instructor as Moderator	Students provided numerous examples of the important role of the instructor, over and above the role of the technology. Instructors must be highly active to facilitate student interaction. Instructor's thorough understanding of the technology was essential or problems crop up. Reproducing the classroom setting using the online technology might miss out on the unique advantages of internet-mediated education.

Memo 6

TO:　　　Fellow Public Administration Teachers

FROM:　　RJS

SUBJECT:　The First Class

Frankly, I find the first class of an introductory course the toughest. Most students in it know little about the subject or your style of teaching, and they may not expect much useful information to emerge from a first session; as a result, they may not be very attentive. Nonetheless, the first class is important because it not only lays out what is going to happen in the weeks ahead but also can serve to establish you as knowledgeable and helpful, an instructor who has valuable ideas to impart during the term.

All teachers have methods for breaking the ice. I like to open the first class by saying, "Okay, gang, this is *not* Art Appreciation 304, but Public Administration 241, and my name is Richard Stillman." Generally, there are some in the class who say, "Gee, I thought this was Art Appreciation 304," and they get up and leave, usually amid laughter. This good-natured kidding captures the students' attention and helps everyone relax.

I then pass out the syllabus and go over it in detail, starting with my office hours. Throughout the initial session, I emphasize that I am available during office hours whenever students need help.

Next I talk about the texts, the course description, and the class objectives, stressing the relevance and challenge of public administration. I try to tell students how public administration touches each of their lives directly, which helps to underscore why they should study the subject. I also insist that there is no one truth about public administration and no single best way to practice it. I want students to know that I am open to their ideas, as long as those ideas are

61

reasonable and logically presented. You might also want to use the Preface to *Public Administration: Concepts and Cases,* Eighth Edition, to outline the approaches and objectives of the class in more detail.

I like to review the grading methods in this first session. It is only fair to make sure that the students understand the grading system, and it is equally important that you follow it consistently throughout the course.

Next I go over the class assignments and briefly discuss the schedule of readings and lectures outlined in the syllabus. It helps students to let them know what the assignments are going to be so that they can plan their schedules accordingly. Be sure to describe the next class assignment explicitly and hand out any necessary supplementary materials. If you plan to include a team project as outlined in Memo 3, go over the project's requirements in detail.

Finally, before the first session ends, I ask the students to prepare, by the next class, short statements about themselves, including their names, a few short sentences about their background, and their addresses, phone numbers, work experiences (if any), and experiences in public administration (if any). I ask them to introduce themselves to others in the class, and I tell them a little about myself as well. The written statements help you get to know your students and give you a record of how to reach them—which is especially useful if group reports are required. The statements are also helpful in preparing a seating chart, which I like to do by the third class meeting so that I can take attendance quickly and call on people by name during class. Knowing the students' names also helps in assigning participation grades fairly. I try to memorize the names by the fourth class, but I usually have to consult the seating chart once in a while throughout the term.

Memo 7

TO: Fellow Public Administration Teachers

FROM: RJS

SUBJECT: Using the Cases

I was lucky enough to have some fine teachers of public administration who were masters at using the case method. Yet I do have unpleasant memories of my first encounter with an administrative case. In my junior year in college my public administration class was assigned a case from the old casebook *Public Administration and Policy Development*, by Harold Stein. The case dealt with the sale of surplus government tankers. In retrospect, I'm certain it was a well-written, insightful case. But I was a college junior with neither background on the general topic nor interest in the subject matter. Very soon after starting this 100-plus-page case, I was lost. Halfway through, I had forgotten the introduction and even why the case had been assigned in the first place. I became hopelessly confused and frustrated, and I soon gave up reading the case.

Needless to say, I survived this first encounter and later became a devotee of the case method. I was converted mainly by my work in the real world of public administration. I learned that a good case gives students a sense of administrative reality that few other classroom exercises can equal, and I now find cases invaluable for teaching administration, as do many renowned teachers in the field.

I also recognize, though, as my first exposure to a case taught me, that cases are not easy to use properly in the classroom, especially where undergraduates new to the field are concerned. As a result, some teachers I know shy away from using them. However, it is not all that hard to learn to use cases well. Professors in law, medicine, and business make a regular practice of teaching with the case method, and so can we.

In *Public Administration: Concepts and Cases*, I have tried to remedy some of the difficulties students and instructors have with the case method. An introduction highlights the key points in each case, the case's relationship to the specific concept under study, and the significant issues students should look for when reading the case. In addition, review questions at the end of each case are meant to ensure that students pick up the key points. I've also tried to select short contemporary cases that are interesting to read and debate.

Still, a lot remains for the teacher to do. Instructors using the text, especially those whose students have never been exposed to public administration or the case method, might want to try the following techniques to help familiarize students with the case method:

1. Emphasize the relevance of the particular case under discussion. Why should students spend their time reading it? Why is this case significant?
2. Go over the basic chronology of facts in the case. What is the basic sequence of events?
3. Highlight the key issues students should discover while reading the particular case. What central problems and dilemmas for the field does it emphasize?
4. Tie the case into the specific concept under review. What answers, if any, does it provide to the precise theoretical questions being addressed?
5. Draw some general *practical* conclusions from the case. On the practical level, what implications and lessons for administrators, or would-be administrators, does it contain?

If the teacher prepares them carefully for analyzing and comprehending cases, I find that most students quickly learn how to handle the case method. Indeed, students can get so excited by a case like "The Blast in Centralia No. 5" that I have trouble moving them on to other things. (I usually start off with a good case like that one to generate enthusiasm and interest in the subject matter.)

In the class discussion, it can help to take an unpopular or contrary point of view just to provoke debate and dialogue; or you can have students with opposite points of view on the case debate each other. These techniques are certain to generate interest and stimulate involvement. Don't worry if you don't thoroughly understand the case yourself or have all the answers to all the problems it poses. One of public administration's attractions is the way solutions evolve through thought and discussion. After the class discussion, you might hand out your own thoughts or other views to provoke further thinking. Such handouts can provoke interesting debate. On pages 73–77 of this memo I have included "An Introduction to the Case Study Method," which offers further tips on the effective classroom use of cases.

For the first few cases that you assign, it may be wise to have students write a one-page summary of what they see as each case's relevance, main facts, key issues, theoretical relationships, and practical lessons. Writing down their ideas in this way helps students grasp the material. This method also ensures that class discussion on the case gets rolling quickly, with everyone participating. On pages 66–72 of this memo you will find three samples of student analyses of major case studies recommended for use in the sample undergraduate and graduate syllabi cited in Memos 2 and 4. Note the various styles and the insights and the conclusions each summary makes about these cases. If the best ones are duplicated and passed out after the case discussion, they can serve as a basis for advancing classroom dialogue and exchange. Another idea is to assign students to "brief" the entire class on the basic facts of the cases prior to discussions, which they can do using overheads or PowerPoint presentations.

Sample Student Analysis 1

CASE ANALYSIS: "THE BLAST IN CENTRALIA NO. 5"

The Problem

The obvious problem with Centralia No. 5 is that an explosion killed 111 people. However, prior to the actual explosion, the problem is less obvious, especially since Centralia No. 5 was similar to so many mines that did *not* explode. In this analysis, I will examine the possible roles and responsibilities of Driscoll O. Scanlan, the mine inspector, *given* the "corruption of modern administrative enterprises" prior to the accident. From this perspective, the perspective of a public official in the field, the problem is that a *potential* danger exists and the regulatory machinery in place to address the danger is ineffective. As an expert, Scanlan recommended that the mine be "dusted" with non-explosive, pulverized stone to diminish the possibility of the coal dust's exploding. However, his expert advice alone was not enough to motivate a response.

History

The chronology of the case shows a progression of "appropriate" action within the existing law and according to organization or bureaucratic norms. On an organizational level, the players include the State of Illinois, the U.S. Government, the Centralia Coal Company, the United Mine Workers of America, and the miners themselves, who could hardly be said to have been well represented by any of the others.

Beginning in 1941, Scanlan's reports of "excessive coal dust" in the Centralia No. 5 mine were sent to Robert Medill, the Director of the Department of Mines and Minerals, and handled as "routine" by Robert Weir, the Assistant to the Director. All three positions were appointed by the Governor, Dwight H. Green. Also in 1941, the U.S. Bureau of Mines began making inspections of mines. The first inspection of Centralia No. 5 was in September 1942. However, only the State of Illinois had any power to enforce compliance, and reports from the Bureau therefore had primary significance as further documentation in the hands of the Department of Mines and Minerals and the Governor. Scanlan's reports were forwarded to the Centralia Coal Company, owned by Bell & Zoller, with a letter requesting that the Company comply with the inspector's recommendations.

Needless to say, the Coal Company did not comply, which is predictable given the lack of any attempt to enforce the requests and the high demand during the war. The mine workers eventually began working through Local Union No. 52, led by William Rowekamp, recording secretary. Throughout the course of events, the mine workers sent correspondence to the State of Illinois, at first to Medill and then directly to the Governor. The letters consistently and emphatically requested attention to the danger present in the mine as documented by Scanlan's extensive reports. The seriousness of the situation seemed to fade within the bureaucratic and political routine within the Department of Mines and Minerals.

Alternatives

Scanlan was faced with several logistical alternatives, but the motivations behind action were of two sorts. As I said before, all of the players followed paths of "appropriate" action within the existing law and according to organizational or bureaucratic norms. The only exception, perhaps, was the Centralia Coal Company. But the coal company clearly recognized a difference between a routine infraction and a serious infraction, at least as it concerned the correspondence from the Department of Mines and Minerals, and they had no indication that Scanlan's reports on Centralia No. 5 were anything unusual. Scanlan's performance was no exception. He did precisely what was required of him by his position. Even the Department itself complied with "the letter of the law." Because the Director of the Department of Mines and Minerals has some discretion, it is not a requirement of law that every technically enforceable infraction *actually* be enforced. This is a matter of judgment.

Scanlan was clearly motivated by attention to law and bureaucratic norms, but he was also pulled by an obvious obligation to the public welfare, in this case the miners' lives at Centralia No. 5. The problem confronting Scanlan was not so much a moral conflict as the need to recognize that compliance with his designated role was inadequate as a response, both as public official and as expert, to the greater responsibility to the public. And because Scanlan's reports were extensive and thorough, including *every* infraction, he had a responsibility to make sure that the decision makers understood the gravity of the danger, perhaps by highlighting the more serious problems.

However, given that the "system" failed to recognize the danger, there were two possible paths of action: (1) work within the system, possibly in ways beyond the designated role of mine inspector; or (2) work outside the system and mobilize public concern, through the union or otherwise. There is a sense in which staying within the system would preserve Scanlan's conformity with legal and organizational norms while still addressing the public welfare. However, there is ample evidence that the organizational players would be unresponsive or at least politically difficult.

Solution

I think that Scanlan could have effected a response within the system, although he would certainly have had to abandon a passive stance. First, the obligation to the general welfare clearly trumps any *mere* compliance with organizational norms and in this case the *spirit* of the law, never mind the letter of the law, is in the name of such general welfare. Second, the role of mine inspectors is to "police the mine operators." This *could* be construed as a responsibility to report infractions and leave enforcement to the Director of the Department. However, because the Director allows his subordinates to handle so much of the "routine," it seems reasonable to expect the inspectors to handle cases like Centralia No. 5 more pro-actively. Third, there is a responsibility left on Scanlan's shoulders as an expert and a professional. His technical expertise allows him to distinguish apparent and real dangers. And because his role in the field puts him in close proximity to the mines, he is perhaps the only individual with such responsibility in a situation where serious problems are apparent.

Costs/Benefits

The costs for Scanlan are evident. Because his position is a "political patronage job," any aggressive pursuit of his responsibilities runs the risk of getting him removed from his position. Of course, this is as much a matter of *how* one negotiates the political terrain as of *what* one is trying to accomplish. I have no doubt that interesting correspondence, emphasizing the prudence of avoiding deaths in the mines, could have been sent to Governor Green, with the assistance and political experience of the Director of the Department of Mines and Minerals, of course.

Even if Scanlan loses his job, the clear benefits are 111 lives. There are hidden benefits as well, though. By generating a relationship with the Director and the Governor, Scanlan is creating a mechanism for handling this sort of issue—a sort of policy formation from below. Given that Centralia No. 5 appears no different from the other mines, this may be the more pressing issue anyway.

Sample Student Analysis 2

"HOW KRISTIN DIED"

Central Issue(s)

The central issue presented is how to respond to and control violent people who threaten specific individuals, particularly in domestic situations. The issue is presented through the case study of Kristin Lardner and her violent ex-boyfriend, Michael Cartier.

Major Factors in Development of Policy/Management Problem

Through the chronological presentation of Kristin's relationship with Michael, its break-up, the involvement of the criminal justice system, and Kristin's eventual murder, the inadequacy of the present system is demonstrated. Elements of the underlying problem include the personal nature of violent relationships, the need for protection of victimized partners, and the difficulty of providing an adequate governmental response. Limiting governmental factors include the commission of crimes in different legal jurisdictions, difficulties of communication and coordination between jurisdictions, overburdened court systems, and an emphasis on protection of defendants' rights. The otherwise worthy goal of using educational/rehabilitative programs to help defendants turn themselves around is contrasted with the difficulty this approach can create for individual victims.

Alternatives for Resolving Problem

Alternatives might include additional funding for domestic violence programs, earlier intervention, help for victims in moving to another geographic area, education for victims about their role in such relationships, an increased focus on the protection of potential victims, harsher sentences for offenders, more effective rehabilitative programs, better coordination of protective services, and education and counseling in schools to help prevent such relationships.

Author's Recommended Solution and Rationale

Without directly saying so, the author suggests that the criminal justice system must become more sophisticated in dealing with violent individuals. The system is viewed as "mindless" because of its inability to respond effectively, or even accurately, to the legitimate needs of citizens. Jurisdictional barriers, inattentive judges, and probation officers who do not take sufficient initiative are among the examples given.

Lessons for Public Administration

This study is an example of a terribly important problem for which government can provide only a limited solution. It illustrates the necessity of carefully defining the goals that government can reasonably hope to achieve and then focusing on improving the delivery of service.

Sample Student Analysis 3

"THE MOVE DISASTER"

The MOVE disaster shows how conflicting values can lead to ineffective management by people of high moral fiber and integrity. For Mayor W. Wilson Goode, "to let deaths occur . . . merely because of noise, stench, code violations, and unpaid utility bills was . . . a morally unbalanced equation" (p. 253 in Stillman, *PA*). But Goode's unwillingness to confront the value conflicts within himself led to what he must have considered a worst case scenario.

The Problem

The problem with MOVE, in a very broad sense, was that Goode faced a "no-win" situation. It seems therefore that Goode needed a defensible strategy based on careful assessment of the situation, *with the clear understanding that no "solution" would be satisfactory.* As it turns out, Goode considered only the most basic responses to the problem and produced a far more *un*satisfactory result than was necessary.

The History

MOVE began in the early 1970s as a group organized around Vincent Leophart and his "anarchistic, back-to-nature philosophy" (p. 242 in Stillman, *PA*). Leophart, who referred to himself as John Africa, developed a "family" who rejected the American lifestyle and refused to cooperate with the system. Throughout the 1970s, John Africa organized passive-aggressive acts of "terrorism" by housing various members of MOVE in houses from which they harassed neighbors and authorities. This pattern culminated in John Africa's establishing MOVE headquarters at 6221 Osage Avenue in Philadelphia.

From this location, MOVE initiated a campaign of "psychological warfare" against their neighbors in order to bring about the release of prisoners by the newly elected mayor, Wilson Goode. After a significant delay in taking action, Goode finally responded with "massive gunfire, deluges of water, and explosive charges [followed by] plastic explosives [dropped] from a helicopter" (p. 241 in Stillman, *PA*).

Alternatives

There were several alternatives available to Goode, each of which would have required that he confront the problem more directly. First, Goode might have developed a long-term anti-MOVE campaign, dedicating genuine problem-solving skills rather than hoping that the situation would resolve itself. Second, Goode might have sought assistance from other professionals (e.g., city managers, psychologists, negotiators), perhaps even hiring a consultant. Finally, Goode might have utilized social/human service agencies to bring about results with respect to more focused objectives, such as protecting the children in the MOVE community.

Solution/Criteria

Given Goode's commitments to protecting both the rights of MOVE members *and* the neighbors affected by MOVE, he should have treated this as a complex problem that could not be handled by simple measures. This required an intelligent long-term solution, for otherwise he would surely "infringe and violate other people's rights in order to achieve the overall good" (p. 252 in Stillman, *PA*). At the same time, recognizing that the immediate problem was a "no-win" situation, Goode nevertheless should have recognized that some aspects *could* be won. Specifically, protecting the children within the MOVE community.

There are several benefits of the less aggressive, long-term "think-tank" strategy with immediate focus on the children: (1) Goode could have avoided any drastic action while claiming that he was in fact doing *something*; (2) deaths would not have been as inevitable as Good surely knew they would be with a raid on the MOVE house; and (3) removing the children would have alleviated some concerns about the risks of violence *and* created some leverage for negotiating with John Africa. The costs would have been the continued nuisance from MOVE members and possible political criticism from the neighbors. But it is not clear how these could have been avoided in any case.

An Introduction to the Case Study Method: Preparation, Analysis, and Participation[*]

Introduction

A case study is a written description of a problem or situation. Unlike other forms of stories and narrations, a case study does not include analysis or conclusions but only the facts of a story arranged in a chronological sequence. The purpose of a case study is to place participants in the role of decision-makers, asking them to distinguish pertinent from peripheral facts, to identify central alternatives among several issues competing for attention, and to formulate strategies and policy recommendations. The method provides an opportunity to sharpen problem-solving skills and to improve the ability to think and reason rigorously.

Most cases depict real situations. In some instances, the data are disguised, and infrequently, the case may be fictional. Cases are not intended to be comprehensive or exhaustive. Most cases are snapshots of a particular situation within a complex environment.

The focus of a case study is on a main protagonist who is shown at the point of a major decision. Typically, the information presented is only what was available to the protagonist in the real situation on which the case is based. Thus, as in real life, important information is often unavailable or incomplete. Because a case study describes reality, it may be frustrating. "Real-life" is ambiguous, and cases reflect that reality. A "right" answer or "correct solution" is rarely apparent.

Although the case study method is principally used in the development and improvement of management skill and leadership ability, its usefulness is not limited to this field. For example, case study pedagogy is also used to teach medical diagnosis to doctors, classroom skills to teachers, and legal decision-making to lawyers. This educational method is useful whenever decision-making must be derived primarily from skillful analysis, choice, and persuasion. The case study method actively engages the participant in these processes: first, in the analysis of the facts and details of the case itself; second, in the selection of a strategy; and third, in the refinement and defense of the chosen strategy in the discussion group and before the class. The case method does not provide a set of solutions, but rather refines the student's ability to ask the appropriate questions and to make decisions based upon his or her answers to those questions.

---

[*] This note was prepared by Sharon A. McDade, Director of the Institute for Educational Management. It was based in part on information included in similar notes on the case method from the Harvard Graduate School of Business Administration, the Institute for Educational Management, and the Institute for Management of Lifelong Education. Copyright © 1988 by the President and Fellows of Harvard College.

Preparation

The case study method is demanding and requires significant preparation time and active class participation. It is intended to build on experiences of the class members and to allow them to learn from one another as well as from the materials and from faculty members. Differences in analysis among participants and faculty members typically arise, and conflicting recommendations emerge as participants with varied perspectives, experiences, and professional responsibilities consider the case.

Preparation of a case for class discussion varies with the background, concerns, and natural interests of participants. In general, it is helpful to follow these steps:

1. Skim the text quickly to establish the broad issues of the case and the types of information presented for analysis.
2. Reread the case very carefully, underlining key facts as you go.
3. Note on scratch paper the key problems. Then go through the case again and sort out the relevant considerations and decisions for each problem area.
4. Prioritize these problems and alternatives.
5. Develop a set of recommendations to address these problems.
6. Evaluate your decisions.

The attached "Suggested Tasks in Analyzing Case Studies" (pp. 76–77) provides a more detailed analysis process.

Another useful educational exercise is to write an analysis of the case. In business, as in many other fields, recommendations are written, even if first presented orally. To enable the reader to quickly focus on important points and to find things within the document without having to read every word, it is best to write a case analysis in outline form, with the liberal use of sub-headings and sufficient tables and charts to illustrate points and relationships.

Participation

Much of the richness of the case study method comes from the class discussion of the cases. The differences which emerge through discussion add richness and dimension to consideration of the issues. It is often helpful to meet with a small number of participants before class to review data, compare analyses, and discuss strategies. This is the time to test and refine your choice of strategies, and to explore and enrich your understanding of the issues in the case through the perspectives of others.

The faculty member's role is to involve many participants in presenting and defending their analyses and recommendations. The faculty member moderates discussion, calling on participants, guiding the discussion, asking questions, and synthesizing comments. Discussion is intended to develop and test the nature and implications of alternate solutions.

The success of a case study depends largely on your active and vigorous participation. Remember to:

- Assert your ideas and prepare to support them.
- Listen to others and evaluate their positions.
- Keep an open mind, yet be willing to change it upon new insights or evidence.
- Make a decision; do not avoid or equivocate.
- Enjoy yourself.

General Notes on Case Studies

A case should seem difficult.   If a case seems difficult, it is invariably because the student is thinking and has recognized a need for additional information. There is no such thing as a state of perfect knowledge and all decisions are made under varying degrees of uncertainty. It is just as important to know what information is missing, and its relative importance, as it is to be able to decide upon a course of action.

All cases are not meant to be alike.   All cases do not require identical emphasis. Many students who enjoy case analyses in one discipline, may be frustrated by cases in another field. In certain disciplines, problem identification and definition alone may be emphasized because of the nature of the discipline; in other fields problems may be elusive but solutions relatively obvious. Development of alternatives may be emphasized to a greater degree in certain other cases.

Suggested Tasks in Analyzing Case Studies

Task	Selected Illustrations in Text	Questions to Ask
Become familiar with case substance	1	What are the facts? What is happening? Is all relevant information available to you?
Determine central issues	2	What decisions need to be made? Who is responsible for making decisions? What factors, issues, and consequences need to be taken into account?
Identify objectives and goals to be achieved	3	Which outcomes are possible? Which are desirable? Which objectives are most important to whom?
Ascertain resources and constraints	4	Which forces support and oppose which actions? Which resources can be marshaled in support of actions? What are the major obstacles?
Ascertain the nature of conflicts	5	What is the substance of conflicts? Can conflicting positions and plans be reconciled?
Identify dynamics of behavior	6	Who is exercising leadership? Are there interpersonal conflicts? Are the persons involved effective in support of their respective positions?
Determine major alternatives	7	Are there ideas and strategies that have not been presented? Is compromise possible? Are the alternatives complementary or mutually exclusive?

Task	Selected Illustrations in Text	Questions to Ask
Assess consequences of likely decisions and actions	8	What actions are likely to result from the decisions made? What unintended consequences might emerge? What are the short and long term consequences for the individuals and the institutions?
Consider appropriate strategies and priorities	9	What are the most effective ways of achieving and implementing the objectives and decisions? Are there intermediate steps or stages?

Memo 8

TO: Fellow Public Administration Teachers

FROM: RJS

SUBJECT: Improving Poor Writing

Before moving onto the specific content of the course, I should discuss another classroom problem facing most college teachers today: poor writing. Obviously there is no simple way to solve this problem, and you certainly can't solve it in one public administration class. But I feel strongly that public administration students today should be encouraged to do as well as they can in preparing written materials for class. You should set high standards from the outset and expect students to try to meet them.

At the beginning of the course, I emphasize my expectations for top-quality reports—both written and oral—and hand out the following "Note on the Mechanics of Paper Writing," which sums up what I feel are the main points of preparing a formal paper. This note is brief but useful for both undergraduates and graduate students, and you might like to use it. I've found that it helps students remember key mechanical aspects of paper writing that many tend to overlook in preparing their reports. I always stand ready, as well, to coach students individually on particular difficulties that they experience in their writing. Usually the combination of high expectations, written reminders, and personal coaching yields pretty good results.

A Note on the Mechanics of Paper Writing

Richard Stillman
Public Affairs Department

Two things about the title above are important. First, this is a *note* and purports to be nothing more. There are books that explore the subject with care; a standard reference is *The Chicago Manual of Style,* published by the University of Chicago Press. Second, this note deals with the *mechanics* of the term paper: It treats neither content nor writing, but only the question of how a term paper should be put together. The suggestions made here do not apply to short exercises, but to substantial pieces of writing—12 or more pages.

1. Introduction

A paper should be typed and double spaced. Occasionally professors may tell you that it's "all right" to submit a paper written in longhand, but don't take them seriously; they'd rather have it typed. *Number the pages.* Where the numbers are placed is optional, but it is good practice to center the number at the bottom of the first page and to place the numbers of subsequent pages half an inch from the top and edge of the paper in the upper right corner.

Break up the material into manageable units. The basic organizational unit is, of course, the paragraph. The length of a paragraph is governed by the thought it covers. As a general rule, half a dozen paragraphs on a page leave the reader breathless, whereas the absence of at least one paragraph break per page can lead to inattention. Paragraphs apart, use an occasional topical heading—one every 3 to 5 pages is a good rule of thumb—to indicate the train of thought.

At this stage in your life, the admonition "write well" is comparable to an exhortation to a violinist to "play well." It is not too late, however, to advise that you exercise all possible care to the end that you write as well as you can; to insist that you allow ample time for writing; or to recommend that you revise, rewrite, and then revise again. Only by constant care can you bring your everyday writing up to its potential.

Beware of familiarities and colloquialisms, except where the text clearly permits such usage. Be careful also of acronyms, which are permissible only when their meaning is clear. At its first usage, spell out an acronym, indicating the abbreviation to be used subsequently: for example, Federal Communications Commission (FCC).

Hold your paper to a reasonable length. In my view, "reasonable length" means 25 to 30 pages *at the most.* If you feel you need to exceed the maximum, please explain why before planning to do so. The length of the paper is controlled most readily by the exercise of care at the three critical stages of organizing, drafting, and revision.

Every paper of substantial length should contain an outline, footnotes, and a bibliography. In addition, it may quite properly carry a number of quotations. It is useful to examine briefly each of these devices.

2. Outline

An outline obviously allows the reader to see what a paper is about. But it serves another and much more important use through its contributions to authorship. Every piece of writing of any substance has an outline for the simple reason that an author cannot proceed past a very superficial presentation without giving at least some thought to the structure of his or her remarks. An outline is much more useful if it is executed as a result of careful and conscientious planning before writing begins.

An outline serves several important purposes. First, it makes explicit the approach to be adopted and the plan to be followed. It compels forethought on both scores. Second, it helps the writer think through the numerous problems, sure to arise, of inclusion and exclusion of material. Third, it assists in attaining both adequate coverage and balance. Fourth, it offers the most important single assurance that the paper will be well organized. Fifth, it helps the writer control length.

The outline is basic in planning and writing a term paper. It is not a proper object for veneration—indeed it can and should be modified as the material and the argument require during writing. At the same time, a careful outline gives the author more help than any other single tool in maximizing the use of the material.

3. Footnotes

FOOTNOTING USAGE.   Footnoting practice varies greatly. A book of almost 200 pages that came to my hand has not more than a dozen footnotes all told. This is permissible in the present instance because the author is a well-known authority who is spinning his personal opinions about a subject with which he is—and is known to be—quite familiar. By contrast, an article of 13 pages that I saw recently had 237 footnotes, which seemed to me to indicate a terrific sense of insecurity or a too-valiant striving for scholarship.

Perhaps it would help to indicate the principal purposes to be served by footnotes. Footnotes should be used to

- indicate the source of every direct quotation incorporated into the text. A citation is also necessary when a passage is paraphrased or its substance is borrowed.

- indicate the authority for every important statement of fact that is not a matter of common knowledge. Footnote references provide a means not only for verifying the writer's statements but also for pursuing a particular question beyond the paper at hand.

- acknowledge each conclusion borrowed or inference drawn from another source.

- discuss or amplify the points that cannot be treated in the text without detracting from the central theme. Footnotes often are used to free the text of descriptions that would interrupt the continuity of the presentation.

FOOTNOTING MECHANICS. Footnotes should be placed at the bottom of the page and numbered consecutively throughout the paper. An alternative system is to group all footnotes at the end of the paper. When footnotes are placed at the bottom of the page, they should be separated from the text by a line of approximately 2 inches drawn from the left margin toward the center of the page. In the body of the text, numbers referring to the footnotes should be placed at the end of the phrase, sentence, or paragraph to which the notes apply. Reference numbers should be raised slightly.

The initial citation of a work should include the full name of the author, the complete title of the work, the name of the publisher, the place and date of publication, and a precise reference to the volume (if any) and page of the source. Although variations are permitted, the following are acceptable standard forms:

For books:

----

[1]Brack Brown and Richard Stillman, *A Search for Public Administration* (College Station, Texas: Texas A&M University Press, 1986), p. 7.

For periodicals:

> [1]James D. Carroll, "Public Administration in the Third Century of the Constitution," *Public Administration Review 47*, no. 1 (Jan./Feb. 1987), pp. 106–114.

For newspapers:

> [1]*The New York Times*, July 26, 2004, 1:1.[*]

For government documents:

> [1]U.S. Senate, *Housing Act of 2002*. Hearing Before a Subcommittee of the Committee on Banking and Currency, U.S. Senate, 85:2, on Various Bills to Amend the Federal Housing Laws, May 14, 2002, p. 286.

FOOTNOTING "SHORTHAND."   When a citation is made to the same work cited in the immediately preceding note, the abbreviation *ibid.* (for the Latin *ibidem*, "in the same place") is used. For example:

> [1]Richard Stillman, *The American Bureaucracy*, 3rd ed. (Belmont, CA: Wadsworth, 2004), p. 103.
>
> [2]Ibid., p. 157.

It is necessary to give the full citation for a work only when it is first cited.

A number of other Latin abbreviations often are used in footnoting. *Op. cit.* is used where references to the same work follow each other closely, but with the intervention of other citations. It means "the work cited." So a reference to *The American Bureaucracy* might be cited

> [1]Stillman, op. cit., p. 140.

If another work by Stillman had intervened between *Bureaucracy* and the next citation of *Bureaucracy*, it would be necessary to repeat the full citation.

Loc. cit. ("place cited") is used if the citation is exactly the same as the one preceding it. *Cf.* is used to direct attention to another passage or statement in the same book or in another work either cited elsewhere in the paper or noted at this point. *Passim* means here and there (in a work). It should be used sparingly.

---

[*] The last item indicates page 1, column 1. This degree of detail is not an absolute requirement.

4. Bibliography

Like footnotes, a bibliography must be compiled with discrimination. A bibliography may be a formal—and formidable—list of all materials discovered relating to a subject. Such a list ordinarily is not of much use. At the other extreme, a bibliography may comprise nothing more than a list of works used in writing the paper at hand. A middle course is represented by a list of works that the author has found useful in the preparation of his or her paper, whether or not every item is cited in a footnote. As is so often the case, the middle course seems the best in normal circumstances.

A bibliography containing more than, say, twenty-five titles should be classified, insofar as possible, according to the character of the works listed. For example, books may be listed in one group, periodicals in a second, and unpublished manuscripts in a third. Interviews are considered bibliography and should be listed.

A bibliography listing is somewhat different from that employed in footnoting. The following are acceptable:

For books:

Stillman, Richard. *The American Bureaucracy.* 3rd ed. (Belmont, CA: Wadsworth, 2004).

For periodicals:

Carroll, James D. "Public Administration in the Third Century of the Constitution." *Public Administration Review 47,* no. 1 (Jan./Feb. 1987), pp. 106–114.

For government documents:

U.S. Senate. *Housing Act of 2002.* Hearing Before a Subcommittee of the Committee on Banking and Currency, U.S. Senate, 85:2, on Various Bills to Amend the Federal Housing Laws, May 14, 2002. Washington, D.C.: U.S. Government Printing Office, 2002.

For interviews:

Wyatt, Ed [Fairfax city manager]. Interview with author. Fairfax, Virginia, July 20, 2001.

5. Quotations

One of the gravest offenses an author can commit is plagiarism—utilizing another author's ideas or data without giving credit. One procedure that ensures integrity is to take the time and trouble to quote accurately from a work of which substantial use is made.

A brief quotation of three typewritten lines or less should be incorporated in the text and enclosed in quotation marks. For example:

> The militia readily put down the uprising, but the revolt sent a shudder down the spines of the most substantial citizens. The outraged General Knox wrote to Washington that "this dreadful situation has alarmed every man of principle and property in New England."[1]

Longer quotations should be set off from the text by indenting and single spacing the passage quoted. Quotation marks are *not* used in this form of quotation. For example:

> The American democratic creed is set forth in succinct and eloquent language in the Declaration of Independence:
>
>> We hold these truths to be self-evident: That all men are created equal; that they are endowed by their Creator with certain unalienable rights; that among these are life, liberty, and the pursuit of happiness.[1]

Omissions of material from a quotation are indicated by ellipsis points. Usually three dots (...) are used, but when the ellipsis occurs at the end of a sentence, the three dots are preceded by a fourth, representing the period. For example:

> The American democratic creed as set forth in the Declaration of Independence rests on the proposition that "... all men are created equal. ..."[1]

PART TWO

The Classes and the Examinations

Memo 9

TO: Fellow Public Administration Teachers

FROM: RJS

SUBJECT: Introducing Public Administration

As these memos indicate, I believe firmly that sound preparation is an important ingredient of successful classroom teaching. If a course is carefully planned and the teacher fully prepares the material, the actual teaching should progress much more smoothly. But teaching itself also demands a lot of work. Therefore, the remainder of this manual offers suggestions that I hope will help you with the actual instruction.

I largely follow the same undergraduate syllabus in Memo 2 in my description of teaching public administration. This memo and the next four memos outline the basic segments there, as follows:

> Memo 9:   Introducing Public Administration
> Memo 10:   Historical, Political, and Legal Development
> Memo 11:   Public Management
> Memo 12:   Public Personnel
> Memo 13:   Public Budgeting

The middle and last weeks of the course are devoted to examinations, and student reports are given during the final two weeks. (Both are dealt with in some detail in the last two memos.) Teachers who don't want to assign student reports can replace them with a concluding segment on ethics and values.

Now let us turn to the first segment. My opening for this segment runs something like this:

> Students, just like consumers of any product, should know what they're getting. After all, we go to great lengths buying a car. We may check *Consumer Reports*, compare prices, and inspect numerous cars on dealers' lots carefully—looking under the hoods and even kicking the tires. Just like an automobile buyer, a student, who consumes knowledge in the classroom (and often pays plenty for it), should study the product. So in the first few classes we are going to do just that sort of thing—provide a prospective buyer—you—with a chance to examine the product—public administration

I then describe public administration as having two dimensions, theory and practice; and I suggest that Dwight Waldo refers to "theorizing or theories about Public Administration" in capital letters and to the actual practice or the processes of public administration in lowercase letters.

To introduce theory, Woodrow Wilson's essay "The Study of Public Administration" is assigned at the end of the first class. Then, during the first two-week segment, we discuss Wilson's background, values, and outlook. I try to let students come up with their own conclusions about the meaning of Wilson's essay. I also have students try to compare themes in a contemporary author's essay to those in Wilson's, with the underlying emphasis that *ideas* are important for determining the substance, purpose, boundaries, and directions of public administration. Students may balk at plunging into theories of public administration at the outset of the course, and many probably won't understand them at first. But I find that by the end of the segment, most students recognize what public administration theory is, how it differs from business administration, its role in society, and the purpose for studying it.

To introduce the practical dimensions, I have students read "The Blast in Centralia No. 5," in Chapter 1. Some teachers have told me that they could build an entire course around this case because of its rich administrative details, complexity, and problems. I certainly think it is an exceptionally good introductory case because of the interest it generates among students.

As I mentioned in Memo 7, I recommend that you guide the class through the first few cases to familiarize the students with case analysis. My introductions to the cases and the review questions can help in this process. One way of introducing "The Blast in Centralia No. 5" is to discuss the leading personalities in the order of their appearance. How were Scanlan, Medill, Green, and the others important to the train of events? You might even ask students to role-play these parts or to analyze what would have happened if one of the principals had behaved differently.

After finishing the case analysis, you might ask the individual members of the class who they think should bear the blame for the accident. The difficulty of assigning responsibility usually generates heated discussion. Tying this debate back to public administration theory, as discussed by Wilson and others, can serve as a good conclusion to the opening segment.

Before discussing particular readings and cases, you may want to ask your students a few questions to see how closely they've read assigned material. Here are some suggestions. Similar questions are provided at the end of Memos 10 through 13.

Pop Quiz

1. Who wrote the first essay on the subject of public administration in America? (*Answer:* Woodrow Wilson)

2. What did Wilson see as the central problem in creating "good" public administration? (*Answer:* Separating "politics" from "administration")

3. Who was the state mine inspector who became a central figure in the case "The Blast in Centralia No. 5"? (*Answer:* Driscoll Scanlan)

4. What prevented Scanlan from closing the mine and making its owners clean it up? (*Answer:* Political pressures)

5. What happened to the miners' "save our lives" letter, sent to Governor Green's attention for his action on their behalf? (*Answer:* Green never saw the letter; it was routed to the Department of Mines and Minerals.)

6. In the end, what was the grand jury's verdict regarding the Centralia Coal Company's responsibility for the explosion? (*Answer:* Two counts of "willful neglect" and a fine of $1,000, or $9 per miner's life lost)

Memo 10

TO: Fellow Public Administration Teachers

FROM: RJS

SUBJECT: The Historical, Political, and Legal Development
                  of Public Administration

The next two weeks are devoted to the historical, political, and legal development of public administration. I normally begin by assigning the Declaration of Independence and the U.S. Constitution. I ask students where these documents mention public administration. After letting the class grapple with this question a while, I point out that although the documents don't mention public administration by name, they contain key concepts that have shaped the development of American public administration. I draw the matrix that appears on the next page on the board, and then we discuss how to define these conceptual elements, how they affect public administration today, and how, if at all, they influenced the outcomes of "The Blast in Centralia No. 5."

Here I also assign *Federalist Papers Nos. 10* and *51* (included on pages 93–101 of this memo) to give students a better idea of what the founders had in mind for the concepts of federalism and the division of power.

The next class session involves a lecture on the development of public service in America. The assigned reading is from Chapter 2 of the text—the Max Weber piece. In the lecture I contrast Weber's "ideal bureaucratic model" with the realities of bureaucratic development as outlined by Stillman in *The American Bureaucracy*, Chapter 2. I use a chalkboard or overhead projector to delineate the lecture's main points, to help the class remember them.

In the next class, we discuss the environmental aspects of administration as specified by the John Gaus and Norton Long readings in Chapters 3 and 4 of the

Key Concepts	Definition of Concept	Effects on Public Administration Today	Influence on the Centralia Case
1. Government of laws			
2. Federalism			
3. Separation of power			
4. Natural rights			
5. Popular sovereignty			

text. Here one can generate lively discussion by having each class member bring in and describe a newspaper article illustrating one of Gaus's or Long's suggestions about how the general environment and politics shape modern administrative activity. These kinds of articles are easy to find, and they expose students to everyday administrative events. This activity also allows each student to speak briefly in class.

The final part of this two-week segment is devoted to analyzing a case that ties together several of Gaus's and Long's ideas about the importance of environmental factors in shaping administrative actions. I like to use "Dr. Helene Gayle and the AIDS Epidemic" in Chapter 3, but almost any case in the text underscores these themes.

Pop Quiz

1. The German social scientist Max Weber discussed the characteristics of what important concept in public administration? (*Answer:* Bureaucracy)

2. Why is the U.S. Constitution so critical to America? (*Answer:* Its basic ideas influence the design, development, processes, and constraints on the public sector.)

3. Name any two of the several ecological factors John Gaus describes that determine development and change in public administration. (*Answer:* People, place, physical technology, social technology, wishes and ideas, catastrophe, and personality)

4. Does Norton Long's essay "Power and Administration" indicate that politics and administration are easily separated? (*Answer:* No)

Federalist Paper No. 10*

Among the numerous advantages promised by a well-constructed Union, none deserves to be more accurately developed than its tendency to break and control the violence of faction. The friend of popular governments never finds himself so much alarmed for their character and fate, as when he contemplates their propensity to this dangerous vice. He will not fail, therefore, to set a due value on any plan which, without violating the principles to which he is attached, provides a proper cure for it. The instability, injustice, and confusion introduced into the public councils, have, in truth, been the mortal diseases under which popular governments have everywhere perished; as they continue to be the favorite and fruitful topics from which the adversaries to liberty deprive their most specious declamations. The valuable improvements made by the American Constitution on the popular models, both ancient and modern, cannot certainly be too much admired; but it would be an unwarrantable partiality, to contend that they have as effectually obviated the danger on this side, as was wished and expected. Complaints are everywhere heard from our most considerate and virtuous citizens, equally the friends of public and private faith, and of public and personal liberty, that our governments are too unstable, that the public good is disregarded in the conflict of rival parties, and that measures are too often decided, not according to the rules of justice and the rights of the minor party, but by the superior force of an interested and overbearing majority. However anxiously we may wish that these complaints had no foundation, the evidence of known facts will not permit us to deny that they are in some degree true. It will be found, indeed, on a candid review of our situation, that some of the distresses under which we labor have been erroneously charged on the operation of our governments; but it will be found, at the same time, that other causes will not alone account for many of our heaviest misfortunes; and, particularly, for that prevailing and increasing distrust of public engagements, and alarm for private rights, which are echoed from one end of the continent to the other. These must be chiefly, if not wholly, effects of the unsteadiness and injustice with which a factious spirit has tainted our public administrations.

By a faction, I understand a number of citizens, whether amounting to a majority or a minority of the whole, we are united and actuated by some common impulse of passion, or of interest, adverse to the rights of other citizens, or to the permanent and aggregate interests of the community.

There are two methods of curing the mischiefs of faction: the one, by removing its causes; the other, by controlling its effects.

There are again two methods of removing the causes of faction: the one by destroying the liberty which is essential to its existence; the other, by giving to every citizen the same opinions, the same passions, and the same interests.

---

* Edward G. Bourne, ed., *The Federalist*, vol. 1 (Washington and London: M. Walter Dunne, 1901), pp. 62–70.

It could never be more truly said than of the first remedy, that it was worse than the disease. Liberty is to faction what air is to fire, an aliment without which it instantly expires. But it could not be less folly to abolish liberty, which is essential to political life, because it nourishes faction, than it would be to wish the annihilation of air, which is essential to animal life, because it imparts to fire its destructive agency.

The second expedient is as impracticable as the first would be unwise. As long as the reason of man continues infallible, and he is at liberty to exercise it, different opinions will be formed. As long as the connection subsists between his reason and his self-love, his opinions and his passions will have a reciprocal influence on each other; and the former will be objects to which the latter will attach themselves. The diversity in the faculties of man, from which the rights of property originate, is not less an insuperable obstacle to a uniformity of interests. The protection of these faculties is the first object of government. From the protection of different and unequal faculties of acquiring property, the possession of different degrees and kinds of property immediately results; and from the influence of these on the sentiments and views of the respective proprietors, ensues a division of the society into different interests and parties.

The latent causes of faction are thus sown in the nature of man; and we see them everywhere brought into different degrees of activity, according to the different circumstances of civil society. A zeal for different opinions concerning religion, concerning government, and many other points, as well of speculation as of practice; an attachment to different leaders ambitiously contending for preeminence and power; or to persons of other descriptions whose fortunes have been interesting to the human passions, have, in turn, divided mankind into parties, inflamed them with mutual animosity, and rendered them much more disposed to vex and oppress each other than to cooperate for their common good. So strong is this propensity of mankind to fall into mutual animosities, that where no substantial occasion presents itself, the most frivolous and fanciful distinctions have been sufficient to kindle their unfriendly passions and excite their most violent conflicts. But the most common and durable source of factions has been the various and unequal distribution of property. Those who hold and those who are without property have ever formed distinct interests in society. Those who are creditors, and those who are debtors, fall under a like discrimination. A landed interest, a manufacturing interest, a mercantile interest, a moneyed interest, with many lesser interests, grow up of necessity in civilized nations, and divide them into different classes, actuated by different sentiments and views. The regulation of these various and interfacing interests forms the principal task of modern legislation, and involves the spirit of party and faction in the necessary and ordinary operations of the government.

No man is allowed to be a judge in his own cause, because his interest would certainly bias his judgment, and, not improbably, corrupt his integrity. With equal, nay with greater reason, a body of men are unfit to be both judges and parties at the same time; yet what are many of the most important acts of legislation, but so many judicial determinations, not indeed concerning the rights of single persons, but concerning the rights of large bodies of citizens? And what are the different classes of legislators but advocates and parties to the causes which they determine? Is a law proposed concerning private debts? It is a question to which the creditors are parties on one side and the debtors on the other. Justice ought to hold the balance between them. Yet the parties are, and must be, themselves the judges; and the most numerous party, or, in other words, the most powerful faction must be expected to prevail. Shall domestic manufacturers be encouraged, and in what degree, by restrictions on foreign manufacturers? are questions which would be differently decided by the landed and the manufacturing classes, and probably by neither with a sole regard to justice and the public good. The apportionment of taxes on the various descriptions of property is an act which seems to require the most exact impartiality; yet there is, perhaps, no legislative act in which greater opportunity and temptation are given to a predominant party to trample on the rules of justice. Every shilling with which they overburden the inferior number, is a shilling saved to their own pockets.

It is in vain to say that enlightened statesmen will be able to adjust these clashing interests, and render them all subservient to the public good. Enlightened statesmen will not always be at the helm. Nor, in many cases, can such an adjustment be made at all without taking into view indirect and remote considerations, which will rarely prevail over the immediate interests which one party may find in disregarding the rights of another or the good of the whole.

The inference to which we are brought is, that the CAUSES of faction cannot be removed, and that relief is only to be sought in the means of controlling its EFFECTS.

If a faction consists of less than a majority, relief is supplied by the republican principle, which enables the majority to defeat its sinister views by regular vote. It may clog the administration, it may convulse the society; but it will be unable to execute and mask its violence under the forms of the Constitution. When a majority is included in a faction, the form of popular government, on the other hand, enables it to sacrifice to its ruling passion or interest both the public good and the rights of other citizens. To secure the public good and private rights against the danger of such a faction, and at the same time to preserve the spirit and the form of popular government, is then the great object to which our inquiries are directed. Let me add that it is the great desideratum by which this form of government can be rescued from the opprobrium under which it has so long labored, and be recommended to the esteem and adoption of mankind.

By what means is this object attainable? Evidently by one of two only. Either the existence of the same passion or interest in a majority at the same time must be prevented, or the majority, having such coexistent passion or interest, must be rendered, by their number and local situation, unable to concert and carry into effect schemes of oppression. If the impulse and the opportunity be suffered to coincide, we well know that neither moral nor religious motives can be relied on as an adequate control. They are not found to be such on the injustice and violence of individuals, and lose their efficacy in proportion to the number combined together, that is, in proportion as their efficacy becomes needful.

From this view of the subject it may be concluded that a pure democracy, by which I mean a society consisting of a small number of citizens, who assemble and administer the government in person, can admit of no cure for the mischiefs of faction. A common passion or interest will, in almost every case, be felt by a majority of the whole; a communication and concert result from the form of government itself; and there is nothing to check the inducements to sacrifice the weaker party or an obnoxious individual. Hence it is that such democracies have ever been spectacles of turbulence and contention; have ever been found incompatible with personal security or the rights of property; and have in general been as short in their lives as they have been violent in their deaths. Theoretic politicians, who have patronized this species of government, have erroneously supposed that by reducing mankind to a perfect equality in their political rights, they would, at the same time, be perfectly equalized and assimilated in their possessions, their opinions, and their passions.

A republic, by which I mean a government in which the scheme of representation takes place, opens a different prospect, and promises the cure for which we are seeking. Let us examine the points in which it varies from pure democracy, and we shall comprehend both the nature of the cure and the efficacy which it must derive from the Union.

The two great points of difference between a democracy and a republic are: first, the delegation of the government, in the latter, to a small number of citizens elected by the rest; secondly, the greater number of citizens, and greater sphere of country, over which the latter may be extended.

The effect of the first difference is, on the one hand, to refine and enlarge the public views, by passing them through the medium of a chosen body of citizens, whose wisdom may best discern the true interest of their country, and whose patriotism and love of justice will be least likely to sacrifice it to temporary or partial considerations. Under such a regulation, it may well happen that the public voice, pronounced by the representatives of the people, will be more consonant to the public good than if pronounced by the people themselves, convened for the purpose. On the other hand, the effect may be inverted. Men of factious tempers, of local prejudices, or of sinister designs, may, by intrigue, by corruption, or by other means, first obtain the suffrages, and then betray the interests, of the people. The question resulting is, whether small or extensive republics are more favorable to the election of proper guardians of the public weal; and it is clearly decided in favor of the latter by two obvious considerations:

In the first place, it is to be remarked that, however small the republic may be, the representatives must be raised to a certain number, in order to guard against the cabals of a few; and that, however large it may be, they must be limited to a certain number, in order to guard against the confusion of a multitude. Hence, the number of representatives in the two cases not being in proportion to that of the two constituents, and being proportionally greater in the small republic, it follows that, if the proportion of fit characters be not less in the large than in the small republic, the former will present a greater option, and consequently a greater probability of a fit choice.

In the next place, as each representative will be chosen by a greater number of citizens in the large than in the small republic, it will be more difficult for unworthy candidates to practice with success the vicious arts by which elections are too often carried; and the suffrages of the people being more free, will be more likely to centre in men who possess the most attractive merit and the most diffusive and established characters.

It must be confessed that in this, as in most other cases, there is a mean, on both sides of which inconveniences will be found to lie. By enlarging too much the number of electors, you render the representatives too little acquainted with all their local circumstances and lesser interests; as by reducing it too much, you render him unduly attached to these, and too little fit to comprehend and pursue great and national objects. The federal Constitution forms a happy combination in this respect; the great and aggregate interests being referred to the national, the local and particular to the State legislatures.

The other point of difference is, the greater number of citizens and extent of territory which may be brought within the compass of republican than of democratic government; and it is this circumstance principally which renders factious combinations less to be dreaded in the former than in the latter. The smaller the society, the fewer probably will be the distinct parties and interests composing it; the fewer the distinct parties and interests, the more frequently will a majority be found of the same party; and the smaller the number of individuals composing a majority, and the smaller the compass within which they are placed, the more easily will they concert and execute their plans of oppression. Extend the sphere, and you take in a greater variety of parties and interests; you make it less probable that a majority of the whole will have a common motive to invade the rights of other citizens; or if such a common motive exists, it will be more difficult for all who feel it to discover their own strength, and to act in unison with each other. Besides other impediments, it may be remarked that, where there is a consciousness of unjust or dishonorable purposes, communication is always checked by distrust in proportion to the number whose concurrence is necessary.

Hence, it clearly appears, that the same advantage which a republic has over a democracy, in controlling the effects of faction, is enjoyed by a large over a small republic,—is enjoyed by the Union over the States composing it. Does the advantage consist in the substitution of representatives whose enlightened views and virtuous sentiments render them superior to local prejudices and schemes of injustice? It will not be denied that the representation of the Union will be most likely to possess these requisite endowments. Does it consist in the greater security afforded by a greater variety of parties, against the event of any one party being able to outnumber and oppress the rest? In an equal degree does the increased variety of parties comprised within the Union, increase this security? Does it, in fine, consist in the greater obstacles opposed to the concert and accomplishment of the secret wishes of an unjust and interested majority? Here, again, the extent of the Union gives it the most palpable advantage.

The influence of factious leaders may kindle a flame within their particular States, but will be unable to spread a general conflagration through the other

States. A religious sect may degenerate into a political faction in a part of the Confederacy; but the variety of sects dispersed over the entire face of it must secure the national councils against any danger from that source. A rage for paper money, for an abolition of debts, for an equal division of property, or for any other improper or wicked project, will be less apt to pervade the whole body of the Union than a particular member of it; in the same proportion as such a malady is more likely to taint a particular county or district, than an entire State.

In the extent and proper structure of the Union, therefore, we behold a republican remedy for the diseases most incident to republican government. And according to the degree of pleasure and pride we feel in being republicans, ought to be our zeal in cherishing the spirit and supporting the character of Federalists.

Federalist Paper No. 51[*]

To what expedient, then, shall we finally resort, for maintaining in practice the necessary partition of power among the several departments, as laid down in the Constitution? The only answer that can be given is, that as all these exterior provisions are found to be inadequate, the defect must be supplied, by so contriving the interior structure of the government as that its several constituent parts may, by their mutual relations, be the means of keeping each other in their proper places. Without presuming to undertake a full development of this important idea, I will hazard a few general observations, which may perhaps place it in a clearer light, and enable us to form a more correct judgment of the principles and structure of the government planned by the convention.

In order to lay a due foundation for that separate and distinct exercise of the different powers of government, which to a certain extent is admitted on all hands to be essential to the preservation of liberty, it is evident that each department should have a will of its own; and consequently should be so constituted that the members of each should have as little agency as possible in the appointment of the members of the others. Were this principle rigorously adhered to, it would require that all the appointments for the supreme executive, legislative, and judiciary magistracies should be drawn from the same fountain of authority, the people, through channels having no communication whatever with one another. Perhaps such a plan of constructing the several departments would be less difficult in practice than it may in contemplation appear. Some difficulties, however, and some additional expense would attend the execution of it. Some deviations, therefore, from the principle must be admitted. In the constitution of the judiciary department in particular, it might be expedient to insist rigorously on the principle: first, because peculiar qualifications being essential in the members, the primary consideration ought to be to select that mode of choice which best secures

---

[*] Edward G. Bourne, ed., *The Federalist*, vol. 1 (Washington and London: M. Walter Dunne, 1901), pp. 353–358.

these qualifications; secondly, because the permanent tenure by which the appointments are held in that department, must soon destroy all sense of dependence on the authority conferring them.

It is equally evident, that the members of each department should be as little dependent as possible on those of the others, for the emoluments annexed to their offices. Were the executive magistrate, or the judges, not independent of the legislature in this particular, their independence in every other would be merely nominal.

But the great security against a gradual concentration of the several powers in the same department, consists in giving to those who administer each department the necessary constitutional means and personal motives to resist encroachments of the others. The provision for defense must in this, as in all other cases, be made commensurate to the danger of attack. Ambition must be made to counteract ambition. The interest of the man must be connected with constitutional rights of the place. It may be a reflection of human nature, that such devices should be necessary to control the abuses of government. But what is government itself, but the greatest of all reflections on human nature? If men were angels, no government would be necessary. If angels were to govern men, neither external nor internal controls on government would be necessary. In framing a government which is to be administered by men over men, the great difficulty lies in this: you must first enable the government to control the governed; and in the next place oblige it to control itself. A dependence on the people is, no doubt, the primary control on the government; but experience has taught mankind the necessity of auxiliary precautions.

This policy of supplying, by opposite and rival interests, the defect of better motives, might be traced through the whole system of human affairs, private as well as public. We see it particularly displayed in all the subordinate distributions of power, where the constant aim is to divide and arrange the several offices in such a manner as that each may be a check on the other—that the private interest of every individual may be a sentinel over the public rights. These inventions of prudence cannot be less requisite in the distribution of the supreme powers of the State.

But it is not possible to give to each department an equal power of self-defense. In republican government, the legislative authority necessarily predominates. The remedy for this inconveniency is to divide the legislature into different branches; and to render them, by different modes of election and different principles of action, as little connected with each other as the nature of their common functions and their common dependence on the society will admit. It may even be necessary to guard against dangerous encroachments by still further precautions. As the weight of the legislative authority requires that it should be thus divided, the weakness of the executive may require, on the other hand, that it should be fortified. An absolute negative on the legislature appears, at first view, to be the natural defense with which the executive magistrate should be armed. But perhaps it would be neither altogether safe nor alone sufficient. On ordinary occasions it might not be exerted with the requisite firmness, and on extraordinary occasions it might be perfidiously abused. May not this defect of an absolute negative be supplied by some qualified connection between this weaker department and the weaker branch of the strong department, by which the latter may be led to support the constitutional rights of the former, without being too much detached from the rights of its own department?

If the principles on which these observations are founded be just, as I persuade myself they are, and they be applied as a criterion to the several State constitutions, and to the federal Constitution, it will be found that if the latter does not perfectly correspond with them, the former are infinitely less able to bear such a test.

There are, moreover, two considerations particularly applicable to the federal system of America, which place that system in a very interesting point of view.

First. In a single republic, all the power surrendered by the people is submitted to the administration of a single government; and the usurpations are guarded against by a division of the government into distinct and separate departments. In the compound republic of America, the power surrendered by the people is first divided between two distinct governments, and then the portion allotted to each subdivided among distinct and separate departments. Hence a double security arises to the rights of the people. The different governments will control each other, at the same time that each will be controlled by itself.

Second. It is of great importance in a republic not only to guard the society against the oppression of its rulers, but to guard one part of the society against the injustice of the other part. Different interests necessarily exist in different classes of citizens. If a majority be united by a common interest, the rights of the minority will be insecure. There are but two methods of providing against the evil: the one by creating a will in the community independent of the majority—that is, of the society itself; the other, by comprehending in the society so many separate descriptions of citizens as will render an unjust combination of a majority of the whole very improbable, if not impracticable. The first method prevails in all governments possessing an hereditary or self-appointed authority. This, at best, is but a precarious security; because a power independent of the society may as well espouse the unjust views of the major, as the rightful interests of the minor party, and may possibly be turned against both parties. The second method will be exemplified in the federal republic of the United States. Whilst all authority in it will be derived from and dependent on the society, the society itself will be broken into so many parts, interests, and classes of citizens, that the rights of individuals, or of the minority, will be in little danger from interested combinations of the majority. In a free government the security for civil rights must be the same as that for religious rights. It consists in the one case in the multiplicity of interests, and in the other in the multiplicity of sects. The degree of security in both cases will depend on the number of interests and sects; and this may be presumed to depend on the extent of country and number of people comprehended under the same government. This view of the subject must particularly recommend a proper federal system to all the sincere and considerate friends of republican government, since it shows that in exact proportion as the territory of the Union may be formed into more circumscribed Confederacies, or States, oppressive combinations of a majority will be facilitated; the best security, under the republican forms, for the rights of every class of citizens, will be diminished, and consequently the stability and independence of some member of the government, the only other security, must be proportionally increased. Justice is the end of government. It is the end of civil society. It ever has been and ever will be pursued until it is obtained, or until liberty be lost in the pursuit. In a society under the forms of which the stronger faction can readily unite and oppress the weaker, anarchy may as truly be said to reign as in a state of nature, where the weaker individual is not secured against the violence of the stronger; and as, in the latter state, even the stronger individuals are prompted, by the uncertainty of their condition, to submit to a government which may protect the weak as well as themselves; so, in the former state, will the more powerful factions or parties be gradually induced, by a like motive, to wish for a government which will protect all parties, the weaker as well as the more powerful. It can be little doubted that if the State of Rhode Island was separated from the Confederacy and left to itself, the insecurity of rights under the popular form of government within such narrow limits would be displayed by such reiterated oppressions of factious majorities that some power altogether independent of the people would soon be called for by the voice of the very factions whose misrule had proved the necessity of it. In the extended republic of the United States, and among the great variety of interests, parties, and sects which it embraces, a coalition of the majority of the whole society could seldom take place on any other principles than those of justice and the general good; whilst there being thus less danger to a minor from the will of a major part, there must be less pretext, also, to provide for the security of the former, by introducing into the government a will not dependent on the latter, or, in other words, a will independent of the society itself. It is no less certain than it is important, notwithstanding the contrary opinions which have been entertained, that the larger the society, provided it lie within a practical sphere, the more duly capable it will be of self-government. And happily for the Republican Cause, the practicable sphere may be carried to a very great extent, by a judicious modification and mixture of the Federal Principle.

Memo 11

TO: Fellow Public Administration Teachers

FROM: RJS

SUBJECT: Public Management

The third segment (which is broken up by the midterm examination) covers public management. As you can see in the syllabus in Memo 2, I spend the first week of this segment on the reading by Rainey and Steinbauer. There are many other excellent managerial approaches and perspectives that could be introduced to new students, but I've decided on Rainey and Steinbauer because it offers good contrasts between public- and private-sector management and provokes lively discussion about public organization effectiveness. Granted, this essay is heavy reading, but it is very influential in modern public management theory, so I feel that students should be exposed to it. In introducing the essay I like to stress the background of management theory. You may also want to trace management theory back to Taylorism and scientific management, which drew almost exclusively on business practices and values. The Rainey and Steinbauer reading provides a useful counterpoint, for it not only is more recent (1999) but also emphasizes the uniqueness of *public* management. Here, of course, the class can debate whether public management is really different and can in fact be made more effective. You might even want to divide the class into a pro side and a con side and have each defend its perspective by preparing a brief position paper.

Once this issue has been thoroughly argued, I turn the class to a case of actual public management. The MOVE case is a good one for this purpose, but there are several other cases pertaining to public management in the text. Whichever one you select, emphasize the enormous complexity of government management and help students reach their own conclusions about its nature and essential attributes

102

today. Why is public management important to society? What are the character-istics of good public managers? How can individuals be prepared for managing government enterprises? What is the best approach to public management? Stress that effective government management is more complex than even Rainey and Steinbauer suggest. Here, too, you might make useful comparisons with "The Blast in Centralia No. 5" and other assigned cases.

As noted, I give a midterm in the sixth week of the course. After that, the course goes into more detail on public management. You might elect to cover two or three of the chapters in Part Two of the text here. I like to discuss decision making (Chapter 8), communications (Chapter 9), and implementation (Chapter 13). Whichever ones you decide to cover, though, it is a good idea to compare and contrast the theoretical readings with one or two cases. I like "The MOVE Disaster" in Chapter 8 because it is controversial and topical, but there are several other excellent cases that can be used here as well.

Pop Quiz

1. Do Rainey and Steinbauer see the tasks of management as being fundamen-tally different for a businessperson than for a government administrator? (*Answer:* Yes)

2. In the case "The MOVE Disaster," what key management problem contrib-uted to the accident? (*Answer:* The mayor's management style)

3. What two methods of decision making are outlined in the essay "The Science of 'Muddling Through,'" by Charles Lindblom? (*Answer:* The root [or com-prehensive] method and the branch [or incremental] method)

4. Does Garnett's essay argue that effective administrative communications are central for making everything else happen in public administration? (*Answer:* Yes)

5. In the case "The MOVE Disaster," what key factors inhibited Mayor Wilson Goode from deciding on, communicating, and implementing an effective plan to remedy the pressing challenges of MOVE? Why did he fail to act? And what would you recommend as *practical* solutions to prevent such problems from reoccurring in the future? (*Answer:* Goode's own psychological problems; "honest" staff feedback)

Memo 12

TO: Fellow Public Administration Teachers

FROM: RJS

SUBJECT: Public Personnel

Public Administration: Concepts and Cases, Eighth Edition, is designed to help you continuously vary the pace of your course by introducing students to a variety of theorists. This varied pace becomes most evident when teaching the personnel segment.

I usually start with a lecture on the five systems of modern public personnel. Here let me encourage you to use Chapter 7 of the eighth edition of *Public Administration: Concepts and Cases*. This chapter outlines the elements of the five systems—political appointments, the professional system, the general civil service, the collective bargaining system, and the contract system. Based largely on that chapter, my lecture covers several aspects of each system: its size, its processes and procedures, its basic values and outlooks, its institutional structures, its present problems, and its future prospects. I also try to find recent news articles that illustrate points I am lecturing about; and I find it helpful to display the matrix that appears on the next page on a chalkboard or overhead projector.

The case in Chapter 11 of the text, "Who Brought Bernadine Healy Down?" also is assigned. This case lends itself to role playing of the major characters. I like to assign groups of students to play the parts because that allows the whole class to participate. Try to make students recognize the relationships between the group role-playing exercise and the workings of the public personnel system.

Personnel leadership and motivation are also dealt with in this segment by assigning Wise's essay in Chapter 11. I know that many public administration instructors may think their concept is too complex. That assessment may be correct,

104

Personnel System	Organization	Size	Procedures	Values	Problems	Prospects
1. Political appointees						
2. Professional system						
3. General civil service						
4. Collective bargaining system						
5. Contract system						

but I use the reading because students with the help of the instructor can grasp its ideas about motivation (which I stress as being a topic central to public personnel) and because it offers good fuel for debate. Normally everyone in class has ideas on the subject of motivation, and Wise's thesis is useful in bringing out students' own views on the topic. You might even ask students to bring to class other contemporary ideas that build on and update motivational theory.

After reading and reviewing these ideas, it is worthwhile to discuss a case study related to the topic, such as Case Study No. 11. This case demonstrates how much more complex and difficult it is to motivate people in the public sector than those in business. Other cases in the text can offer plenty of good topics for discussion on public personnel, among them employees' rights, the role of the courts, problems of lower-level public servants, supervision, grievance processes, community interest, media attention, and business regulation.

Pop Quiz

1. Stillman's essay in Chapter 7 argues that within every established profession there is a key, controlling group. What does he call that group? (*Answer:* The professional elite)

2. Give one example of an established public profession at the federal level. (*Answer:* Military officers, diplomatic service, public health officers)

3. Why are political appointees critical to government? (*Answer:* To provide top-level policy direction)

4. In what specific way is contract employment changing public administrators' roles? (*Answer:* By making public administrators become contract managers rather than traditional line managers)

Memo 13

TO: Fellow Public Administration Teachers

FROM: RJS

SUBJECT: Public Budgeting

Unquestionably many students view public budgets and finance as the driest, least appealing segment of an introductory public administration course. Yet students should be impressed from the start of this segment that budgets are the heart of modern public administration. The allocation of money is central to public-sector activities, and a successful public administrator must understand the realities of the budget process. Although I don't agree, some in the field believe that today public budgets and public administration are one and the same.

As you impress on students the importance of this topic, you also have to indicate that you can offer them only a brief overview of the subject. In this short period, they cannot become experts; but you should try to teach them why this topic is so critical to modern public administration.

You might start by showing students an actual budget—any local, county, or state budget or the summary portion of the federal budget will do. I also like to begin the segment with a guest speaker—a knowledgeable budget practitioner—who can discuss the nature of modern public budgeting and underscore its importance in government. These two activities at the outset tend to stimulate students' interest in a topic that they may find uninviting at first.

I assign Irene Rubin's "The Politics of Public Budgets" from Chapter 12 of the text, and we next have a discussion on the various uses of budgets in government—that is, for accountability, as a management tool, for planning, for making political choices, and for fiscal and policy development. We also discuss the roles of the various players in the budgetary process as outlined by Rubin. Here, too, I like to

107

draw out the class, letting the students themselves arrive at conclusions about the roles of budgets and budgeters in modern government. As well, using the matrix on the next page, I give a brief lecture on the formal cycle of budget development in government.

In addition, I either hand out or show on an overhead projector samples of four types of budgets—line item, performance, PPBS, and ZBB—and then discuss the elements of the various formats, their underlying rationales, and their impact on government. [These four types of budgets are discussed in Part III of my *Basic Documents of American Public Administration Since 1950* (New York: Holmes and Meier, 1982).]

The remainder of the segment is given over to discussing a recent case of budgeting in action, James K. Conant's "Wisconsin's Budget Deficit" (in Chapter 12 of the text). The case fits nicely with Rubin's conceptual writing about the roles, strategies, politics, and processes of contemporary budgeting. The case should be clear and easy for students to grasp. Here, again, role-playing the characters in the case can add interest.

Pop Quiz

1. In Rubin's view, are public budgetary decisions made by one person, a few actors, or many "decision clusters"? (*Answer:* Many decision clusters)

2. How does "macrobudgeting" differ from "microbudget analysis"? (*Answer:* The former deals with "big picture" issues of budget policymaking.)

3. What federal agency is principally charged with developing and presenting the president's budget for the executive branch? [*Answer:* The Office of Management and Budget (formerly the Bureau of the Budget)]

4. What are budget strategies? (*Answer:* Budget participants' activities designed to secure their budgetary goals)

5. In the case "Wisconsin's Budget Deficit," how did they succeed in formulating a compromise budgetary strategy? (*Answer:* By using an incremental strategy)

Phases of Budgeting	Period	Purpose	Actors Involved	Sources of Possible Conflict and Means for Resolution
1. Executive preparation phase				
2. Legislative approval phase				
3. Executive implementation phase				
4. Audit and review phase				

Memo 14

TO: Fellow Public Administration Teachers

FROM: RJS

SUBJECT: The Final Session

As outlined in Memos 2 and 3, I favor using the last few weeks for student reports. For various reasons cited earlier, I believe they are valuable exercises, particularly in public administration courses. You may decide otherwise, though. If so, alternatives for filling the remaining weeks include discussions of the ethical problems of public administration (Chapter 16 of the text).

Whatever you choose to cover during this period, the course should end with a final review session so that students can integrate what they have learned during the term. The specific points you cover in this session depend, of course, on what went on during the semester or quarter in your class, but it is important to give students an idea of what they should concentrate on in studying for the final exam. I always urge them to ask me questions about points in the readings, discussions, and lectures that were not clear to them. I also hand out sample exam questions to indicate the type and format of the examination. And I encourage the students to study together in small groups. In groups, able students help the not so able ones, and this sharing raises the common level of knowledge. (Much of what appears here about preparation applies to both midterm and final exams.)

At the end of the review session, I pass out a course evaluation form. Evaluation forms are controversial topics at most colleges and universities. In some cases, instructors are required to use certain forms in specific ways and at specific times. In others, where evaluations are optional, let me suggest that you develop your own instrument, geared to your needs, your style of teaching, and your course content. (The problem I find with most standard evaluation forms is that they are not germane to every instructor's style or subject.)

I think an evaluation that gives regular feedback from students can help an instructor improve. It can help indicate what parts of a course worked well or poorly and, perhaps, how the instructor can correct mistakes. Also, course evaluations can give students a sense of participating in improving the course for future students. Course evaluation forms also provide evidence of your classroom performance, should you ever need it to further your career.

To conduct a successful course evaluation:

1. Develop an instrument tailored to your teaching style and subject matter.
2. Introduce the instrument by telling students you genuinely want their feedback to make the course better.
3. Tell them also to be *specific* in their comments about what should be improved. You don't want statements like "You're a poor teacher." Rather, ask students to state exactly what they disliked about the course and what changes need to be made.
4. Give students adequate time to complete the evaluation form in class, or let them take it with them and mail it back to you.
5. To assure students that their evaluations will not influence their grades, give them the option of not signing the form.
6. Leave plenty of room on the form for qualitative feedback so that students can air their personal feelings about your teaching practices.

A sample course evaluation form follows.

Sample Evaluation Form

TO: Members of the MPA Class

FROM: Professor Richard Stillman

SUBJECT: Feedback on the MPA Seminar

I need your help in planning my next MPA course. Your experience is a vital indicator of what went well and what went badly in this one. I have prepared this instrument to solicit honest, critical, constructive opinions from you about the conduct of the course. Feel free to sign the instrument or not. Please return it to me after you have completed it.

1. Readings

    a. The amount of reading assigned was reasonable for MPA-level work (check one).

Strongly Disagree	Disagree	Neutral	Agree	Strongly Agree

    b. The strong emphasis on primary seminal works was appropriate.

Strongly Disagree	Disagree	Neutral	Agree	Strongly Agree

    c. The sequence of reading was appropriate to the development of the subject matter.

Strongly Disagree	Disagree	Neutral	Agree	Strongly Agree

Comments:

2. Research Projects and Papers

   a. The writing standards set for the course were fair, consistent, and appropriately high.

Strongly Disagree	Disagree	Neutral	Agree	Strongly Agree

   b. Appropriate materials and research guidance for papers (for example, handouts, examples, library orientation) were provided by the instructor.

Strongly Disagree	Disagree	Neutral	Agree	Strongly Agree

   c. The papers and projects assigned aided in the understanding of the information, the ideas, and the importance of public administration subjects.

Strongly Disagree	Disagree	Neutral	Agree	Strongly Agree

   Comments:

3. Exercises

    a. The task force project was a good learning device.

Strongly Disagree	Disagree	Neutral	Agree	Strongly Agree

    b. The instructor offered enough help on the project.

Strongly Disagree	Disagree	Neutral	Agree	Strongly Agree

    c. Sharing research results orally in class was a valuable learning experience.

Strongly Disagree	Disagree	Neutral	Agree	Strongly Agree

    d. The group or team approach to the research project was a valuable learning experience.

Strongly Disagree	Disagree	Neutral	Agree	Strongly Agree

    Comments:

4. Guest Speakers

    a. The choice and number of guests were relevant to the learning objectives of the MPA class.

Strongly Disagree	Disagree	Neutral	Agree	Strongly Agree

Comments:

5. Course Lectures, Content, and Procedures

a. Lectures by the instructor and class discussions were valuable for understanding the material.

Strongly Disagree	Disagree	Neutral	Agree	Strongly Agree

b. Synopses (individual summaries) of case materials were a helpful way to study and share insights about the case under review.

Strongly Disagree	Disagree	Neutral	Agree	Strongly Agree

c. Small-group work and role-playing exercises were useful ways to organize class participation and learning.

Strongly Disagree	Disagree	Neutral	Agree	Strongly Agree

d. Transitions and linkages between the subjects were adequately indicated by the instructor.

Strongly Disagree	Disagree	Neutral	Agree	Strongly Agree

e. Course descriptions outlined in the syllabus were reasonably clear, complete, and helpful in understanding the material.

Strongly Disagree	Disagree	Neutral	Agree	Strongly Agree

f. The midterm and final examinations were fair, relevant, and suitably challenging.

Strongly Disagree	Disagree	Neutral	Agree	Strongly Agree

Comments:

6. Open-ended Questions

a. Did your experience in the course change your initial perspectives about public administration?

b. Comment briefly on what things went particularly well in class and should be continued or emphasized.

c. Comment briefly on what things went badly and should be done better or eliminated.

d. What specific elements of the course would you recommend be changed in the future?

Memo 15

TO: Fellow Public Administration Teachers

FROM: RJS

SUBJECT: Midterm and Final Examinations, as well as using cases
            in other classes

There are many approaches to developing exams. My view is that exams should be seen as a way to prod students to understand and integrate the material presented in a course and to gauge how well they have mastered it. What goes into an exam, then, should be determined by what you want your students to learn from your course. If you clearly define your aims and objectives from the start, students should respond well to your exams.

Although my objective for exams may not be the same as yours, I feel that all exams should be announced in class ahead of time and described so that students know what to expect. I indicate early in the course that I give exams for the following reasons:

- To foster the integration of the material studied in the course
- To encourage students to develop their own ideas, opinions, and reactions regarding these materials
- To improve the students' writing, reasoning, and analytical skills
- To provide me with solid evidence of what students have learned from the course so that I can grade their efforts accordingly (although exams are just one of the indicators I use in assigning final grades)
- To challenge students to solve problems creatively on paper

I also add that my midterm exam should give them an idea of what to expect on the final. I use the midterm to show students my exam style so that there will be, I hope, no surprises on the final. And I spend considerable class time reviewing students' mistakes on the midterm exam.

I like to tailor each exam to the specific progress of a course. To this end I keep a course journal; and after each class session, I note the issues discussed, the points raised, and associated questions that would be suitable for the midterm or final. I review these notes a week or so before making up the exam. They help me prepare an exam geared to the special interests and ideas of the class.

I've never given an objective-question exam. I feel that public administration does not lend itself to questions with simple right and wrong answers. Instead I prefer an exam format that balances short-answer and essay questions. For the short-answer questions, I ask students to write a sentence or two about the meanings of key terms covered in the course to make certain they have done their reading and paid attention in class. The essay questions cover important issues that have been discussed in class or in the text and require students to integrate and analyze diverse ideas. I give students a choice of both key-term and essay questions. (See the sample midterm and final exams that follow.) The key terms can be conveniently drawn from the end of each chapter in *Public Administration: Concepts and Cases,* Eighth Edition, and the questions there can help in formulating essay questions.

Finally, I've been asked how *Public Administration: Concepts and Cases,* Eighth Edition, can be adapted for use in teaching other classes. On pages 128–132 of this memo I have included a class syllabus I regularly use for teaching Leadership and Professional Ethics. Note how cases are assigned weekly to promote class debates in relationship to the required readings. This course has turned out to be one of the most exciting *and* popular in our program.

This concludes my comments and suggestions, which I hope will be of help. Good luck with your endeavor to teach public administration. And please write to me if you have any ideas about how to teach better, or if you have questions about the text or this manual. I certainly don't have all the answers for effectively teaching public administration. I'm still learning!

Professor Richard J. Stillman
Graduate School of Public Affairs
University of Colorado, Denver
Campus Box 142, P.O. Box 173364
Denver, CO 80217
Phone: (303) 556-5970
Email: Richard.Stillman@cudenver.edu

Sample Midterm Exam
for an Introductory Undergraduate Course

INTRODUCTION TO PUBLIC ADMINISTRATION

Government 241
Midterm Exam

1. Identify *four* of the following eight terms in brief, two- or three-sentence descriptions.

    Woodrow Wilson   public management
    public bureaucracy   administrative power
    legal-rational authority   separation of powers
    ecology of administration   interest groups

2. Answer *one* of the following two essay questions.

    a. During the first week of class we wrestled with the problem of understanding the scope and substance of public administration. We learned that because public administration is so pervasive, touching all our lives directly or indirectly, it is very difficult to define precisely. Nevertheless, in the case study by John Bartlow Martin, "The Blast in Centralia No. 5," we can glimpse some of the realities about the contemporary nature of public administration.

        Discuss what this case reveals about the following issues: (1) What is public administration? (2) How does public administration differ from business administration? (3) What central problem(s) does the field face? (4) How can we respond to the problem(s) realistically and effectively?

    b. "Over the years we have moved from *one best way* to *many best ways* to manage public agencies. The challenge for contemporary public managers is finding and then applying an effective method for public management."

        Discuss this statement in relation to the public management essay we analyzed in Rainey and Steinbauer's "Galloping Elephants." What is the central idea of their essay? Do you agree that achieving effective public management is possible? Why or why not? What is "effectiveness," in their view?

Sample Final Exam
for an Introductory Undergraduate Course

INTRODUCTION TO PUBLIC ADMINISTRATION

Government 241
Final Exam

Answer each of the following six questions (each question counts 16-2/3%).

1. Identify *four* of the following eight terms by writing one- or two-sentence definitions.

"root method" of decision making	fiscal year
professional elites	GS rating
classification of positions	GAO
line-item budgets	merit system

2. This semester each of you served on a team that studied a major professional group in American government. In many respects this exercise demonstrated the dilemma faced by modern public administration—namely, the difficulties of organizing a group of people to achieve specific results in a limited period of time.

   How do you plan a project successfully? Implement a plan effectively in a limited time? Gain cooperation from uncooperative individuals? Motivate and lead people? Each of you faced all of these problems and many more in putting together your team's oral and written reports. Outline the major lessons you learned from this exercise in public administration. What do you think you did successfully in organizing this exercise? What would you do differently if you could do the project over again? Be specific in your answer.

3. We heard two outstanding guest speakers in this class: _____ and _____. Compare and contrast the scope of their duties, roles, and responsibilities as they described them to us in class. Specifically outline how their work differs. Where do their activities overlap? Where are they similar? Be specific in your answers, drawing illustrations from the speakers' lectures.

4. Answer *either* a or b.

    a. The nature of the contemporary public personnel system consists of five
        personnel subsystems:

        (1) Political appointments
        (2) Professional system
        (3) General civil service
        (4) Collective bargaining system
        (5) Contract system

        Select *two* of these subsystems and compare and contrast their size,
        composition, functions, key elements, and basic values, as well as major
        problems that currently exist within them.

    b. "The Decision to Go to War in Iraq," Case 7, illustrates the prominent
        role public professionals play in deciding critical issues in public
        administration. Who were the key professionals in this case? How did
        they exercise their influence? How would you judge their effectiveness,
        and why would you use these criteria?

5. Answer *either* a or b.

    a. Various theories or models of decision making are prominent in academic
        literature today. Two are especially important to public administration:

        (1) The comprehensive model
        (2) The incremental model

        Describe the basic elements of each model as well as the pros and
        cons of each one. Which one do you think is the more effective decision-
        making model? Why?

    b. "The MOVE Disaster" describes a difficult choice faced by a public offi-
        cial in America—one that we hope will never have to be faced again.
        Outline the chronology of events that led up to the decision to use the
        police against MOVE, particularly the critical decisional factors that
        led to the use of force. How did Mayor Goode resolve the key issues he
        faced? In your opinion, did he decide these issues wisely and effec-
        tively? Why or why not? If you had been in Goode's position, would you
        have made any of these choices differently? If so, which ones and why?
        What model of decision making did Goode use—comprehensive,
        incremental, or what . . . ?

6. Answer *either* a or b.

   a. The budget cycle is divided into four phases. Discuss each phase in detail, explaining its sequence and duration, its basic function, and its importance to the budgetary cycle. Identify the major people and agencies involved with each phase, as well as the conflicts that may be generated in each phase.

   b. The case "Wisconsin's Budget Deficit" points out the importance of the political aspects of the budgetary process. Who were the major "players" in this case? What budgetary strategies did they pursue? Why did they pursue them? What ultimately determined the "outcomes"? Who were the "winners" and "losers," and why?

Sample Midterm Exam
for an Introductory Graduate Course

THEORY AND PRACTICE OF PUBLIC ADMINISTRATION

PUAD 502
Midterm Exam

1. Identify with one- or two-sentence definitions *four* of the following eight terms (counts as 1/3 of the exam).

   natural rights   government corporation
   federalism   BoB Circular A-95
   bureaucracy   Kestenbaum Report
   social technology   Taft Report

2. Answer *one* of the following two essay questions (counts as 2/3 of the exam).

   a. Discuss the *major* factors that led to the mine explosion in the case "The Blast in Centralia No. 5." What does this case say about the difficulties of fixing or assigning responsibility in public administration?

   b. As the essay by Hugh Heclo, "Issue Networks," points out, the problem of finding the appropriate relationship between politics and administration has become, once again, a significant issue in the 1990s. Outline the *major* approaches formulated since Woodrow Wilson's essay (1887) that seek to resolve this issue, and describe specifically how the case "Reinventing School Lunch" points out the contemporary difficulties of effectively relating political oversight to administrative action.

Sample Final Exam
for an Introductory Graduate Course

THEORY AND PRACTICE OF PUBLIC ADMINISTRATION

PUAD 502
Final Exam

Each question counts as 1/6 of the exam.

1. Identify with one- or two-sentence definitions *six* of the following eleven terms.

Civil Service Act of 1883	Budget and Accounting Act
professional career system	of 1921
OPM	GAO
professional elites	budget cycle
Merit System Protection Board	CBO
inspector general's office	OMB

2. This term each of you examined a major legislative act, commission report, or executive order that served as a fundamental building block for modern American public administration. Discuss the lessons you learned from this firsthand administrative research, specifically in terms of how a careful study of administrative documents is useful to administrative practitioners or would-be administrative practitioners. What is the value of this kind of research for learning about public administration both as a field of study and as a professional calling? In other words, generalize about the worth of your research endeavor with regard to your future career and your intellectual understanding of the subject.

3. As you prepared the report mentioned in Question 2, each of you served on a task force organized to carry out the project. In several respects this exercise demonstrated many of the problems of modern public management: namely, how to plan, organize, communicate, coordinate, and implement group activity to achieve some common task (in this case, an oral and a written report). Reflect on your task force experience from an "administrative" standpoint. What lessons about public administration did you learn from this exercise?

What went well in organizing your task force assignment? What went poorly? What would you do differently if you had the whole project to do over again? Be specific.

4.   Answer *either* a or b.

   a.   Frederick C. Mosher argues that "for better or worse—or better and worse—much of our government is now in the hands of professionals." Why does Mosher make this assertion? What are the consequences or problems that have resulted from the rise of public professionalism? How can we make certain that professionals are indeed responsive to the public interest? Discuss the mechanisms that are or ought to be in place to ensure professional responsibility to the public.

   b.   The Civil Service Reform Act of 1978 was the first major reform of the federal civil service since its inception in 1883. Discuss some of the significant changes that this act introduced and the major problems that these reforms raise today with regard to civil service practices at the federal level.

5.   Answer *either* a or b.

   a.   Analyze Irene Rubin's essay "The Politics of Public Budgets" from the standpoint of what it has to say about (1) the key "decision clusters" in the budgetary process; (2) the major strategies the players utilize in each decision cluster; (3) the key sources of conflict among players; (4) the importance of macro and micro budgetary approaches; and (5) the differences between private and public budgetary processes. Do you believe Rubin accurately describes today's public budgetary processes? Why or why not?

   b.   The budget cycle is divided into four phases. Discuss the purpose of each phase, its sequence and duration, the players involved in each phase, the sources of conflict engendered in each phase, and the problems—both institutional and political—encountered in each phase.

6.   Answer *either* a or b.

   a.   A number of important reforms were adopted in the 1970s at the federal, state, and local levels to improve bureaucratic responsiveness and oversight. What were some of these major accountability reform measures? Why were they enacted? Overall, what results have been achieved by these reforms, specifically in terms of administrative processes? How do the reforms of the 1970s look from the standpoint of the administrative demands and challenges of today?

b. Both "The Blast in Centralia No. 5" and "Dr. Helene Gayle and the AIDS Epidemic" have much to say about the difficulty of securing administrative responsibility and responsiveness. Compare and contrast these two cases, especially in terms of the actions (or inactions) of the principal actors as they carried out their assigned administrative duties. What do both cases tell us about the problems of ensuring responsible action on the part of public officials? In the future, what do you recommend should be done to secure responsible official behavior?

Sample Ethics/Leadership Syllabus

University of Colorado at Denver
Graduate School of Public Affairs

LEADERSHIP AND PROFESSIONAL ETHICS
PAD 5006/7006

Professor: Richard Stillman
Place: TE 116
Time: Wednesdays, 6:55–9:35 P.M.
Office Hours: Wednesdays, 3 to 5 P.M.,
      and a half hour before
      and after class

Office Phone: 556-5982 or
GSPA Phone: 556-5970
GSPA Fax: 556-5971
Email: Richard.Stillman@
      cudenver.edu

The goals of this graduate seminar on leadership and professional ethics are four-fold: first, to improve student proficiency at case analysis. Each week class members will be asked to prepare a *one-page* synopsis of an assigned case (no late papers will be accepted). The cases will be drawn from a range of contemporary leadership and ethical problems facing public administrators from Stillman's *Public Administration: Concepts and Cases,* Eighth Edition. Student one-page summaries should focus on such issues as what are the central leadership and ethical issue(s) in the assigned case? the major factors contributing to the development of the problem under review? the alternatives for resolving the problem? the writer's recommended solution as opposed to how the case was actually resolved? the criteria and rationale(s) for the proposed remedy? the significance or "lessons" for ethical leadership? By this exercise of repeated case analysis, hopefully class members can increase their sensitivity to the complex administrative ethical problems, improve their leadership skills, sharpen their capacity to see the range of creative solutions available to an administrative problem, as well as better appreciate the various "outcomes" that are inherent in the alternative options.

    A second class objective will be to study major biographies of famous leaders and "anti-leaders" drawn from Gary Wills, *Certain Trumpets* (as well as chapters from John Gardner's *On Leadership* related to themes of ethical leadership). Each week, in conjunction with the assigned case, the instructor will appoint teams of students to lead a 30-minute class discussion on one leader and one anti-leader under review. These leaders and anti-leaders can help us understand various types of models that influence the way we think about modern ethical leadership in the United States. The oral presentations should be *critical* reviews and address such questions as what are the major ethical and leadership themes presented in each biography? their relationship to the Gardner reading? the "lessons" for practitioners? the values and prescriptions for public administration? potential implications for aiding our understanding of ethical leadership? the pros and cons of that particular leadership model? This segment may also give students a deeper appreciation of the key figures and their ideas that contribute to the thinking about ethical leadership today—as well as into the future.

The third goal of this class will be to look carefully at contemporary professions in government. The assumption behind undertaking this exercise is that modern public service ethical leadership is largely defined by and controlled by professions, namely their ethical codes, associations, educational standards, etc. Every student will be asked to select *one* (ideally related to his/her chosen career interests) professional group, research that *one* profession in government in depth and prepare an oral report on how its ethical and leadership values and norms are framed: by codes of conduct? professional association standards? senior role models? or what? Oral reports will be due by the end of the class. The optional professions for study and the topics to be addressed will be explained in the first class meeting. Choices for topics will be requested by the second class meeting. Students will be given time in class and guidance from the instructor for preparing this professional study assignment. By the 5th week, students will be asked to give *oral* reports on their research *and* any problems they encounter. The aim of this exercise is to provide students with a better understanding of how contemporary professions shape the content, direction, and purposes of ethics and leadership in the public sector as well as a better appreciation of the complexities of ethical leadership. By discussing "the findings" of these reports at the end of the class, perhaps some generalizations can be made about the dynamics and nature of how professions shape ethical leadership practices today.

The fourth goal is to use journaling as a method of integrating your *own* thinking on ethics and leadership. Each student will be asked to keep a personal journal in which he or she records at least once each week his or her ideas, observations, and reflections on ethics and leadership. These notes may be from in-class readings, discussions, or outside experiences, such as from current events on TV or in the newspapers, or by watching a film. A sample of the sort of film summary might be as follows:

> "The Last Emperor"—Directed by Bernardo Bertolucci—1987
>   John Lone—Emperor Pu Yi
>   Joan Chen—Empress
>   Peter O'Toole—Reginald Fleming-Johnston

> The question which arises when looking for the development of ethical leadership in "The Last Emperor" is, "What will followers do to make the child Emperor a leader?" The answer is nothing. The boy is the last

of his line. He is not to be a leader, but a symbol of the old way. As Pu Yi becomes educated, he begins to seek responsibility and leadership without knowing what it is. He believes he has become a leader when the Japanese give him Manchuria, only to find he is just a puppet of a different master. This film is a sensitive portrayal of the life of a man who is kept in ignorance as the world changes around him, but it has little to say about leadership.

At the end of the class, meetings with students and the instructor will be arranged to "debrief" on what you learned from this "journaling experience" and how you developed *your own thinking about ethical leadership*. The aim of this exercise ultimately is to help each student clarify and integrate his/her own ethical leadership values.

Grading

There will be *no* mid-term or final exams. Grades will be based on:

25%—Written one-page case summaries
25%—Oral presentations and discussions on books
25%—Oral report on a profession in government
25%—Personal Journal on Ethical Leadership

Required Books

John W. Gardner, *On Leadership* (NY: Free Press, 1990), paper.

Nicolo Machiavelli, *The Prince* (Chicago: U. of Chicago Press, 1985), paper.

James Madison, Alexander Hamilton, John Jay, *The Federalist Papers* (NY: Mentor, 1961 edition), paper.

Richard Stillman, *Public Administration: Concepts and Cases*, 8th ed. (Boston: Houghton Mifflin Co., 2004), paper.

Gary Wills, *Certain Trumpets* (NY: Simon & Schuster, 1994).

"*Order of March*"

1st Week: Introductions, assignments, etc. By the second class, please hand in a one-page résumé with your name, address, phone, etc.

2nd Week: The Great Western Debate over Ethical Leadership and The Rise of the Professional State as well as Alternative Ethical Leadership Constructs for Public Service
Readings: Dwight Waldo's "Public Administration and Ethics" in Stillman's *Public Administration,* Chapter 16, as well as Machiavelli's *Prince* and Madison, Hamilton, and Jay's *Federalist Papers,* nos. 10, 23, 37, 39, 47, 48, 51, 67–70

3rd Week: Individual group meetings with instructor

4th Week: Ethical Leadership Perspectives from Constitutional Leaders
Readings: John Gardner's *On Leadership,* Chapters 1 and 2, Gary Wills, *Certain Trumpets,* Chapter 9
Ethical Leadership Dilemmas from Administrative Inaction
Case: "The Blast in Centralia No. 5," in Stillman, Chapter 1

5th Week: Ethical Leadership Ideas from Radical Leaders
Readings: Gardner, Chapters 7 and 12; Wills, Chapter 2
Ethical Leadership Dilemmas from Political Micromanagement
Case: "The Columbia Accident," in Stillman, Chapter 4

6th Week: Ethical Leadership Viewpoints from Reform Leaders
Readings: Gardner, Chapters 3 and 4; Wills, Chapter 3
Ethical Leadership Dilemmas from Conflicting Political Interests
Case: "The Decision to Go to War in Iraq," in Stillman, Chapter 7

7th Week: Progress Reports on Professional Research Assignments (each student will present a brief "overview" of his/her own research to date, including outlines, interviews, primary sources used, issues and problems involved in completing the study)

8th Week: Ethical Leadership of Elected Leaders
                   Readings: Gardner, Chapters 5 and 6; Wills, Chapter 1
                   Ethical Leadership Dilemmas over What to Tell the Media
                   Case: "The Shootings at Columbine High School," in
                       Stillman, Chapter 9

9th Week: Ethical Leadership from Diplomatic Leaders
                   Readings: Gardner, Chapters 9 and 10; Wills, Chapter 4
                   Ethical Leadership Dilemmas from Divided Personal Values
                   Case: "The MOVE Disaster," in Stillman, Chapter 8

10th Week: Ethical Leadership Knowledge from Business Leaders
                   Readings: Gardner, Chapters 8 and 13; Wills, Chapter 7
                   Resolving Ethical Leadership Dilemmas Through Creative
                       Action
                   Case: "The Human Genome Project," in Stillman, Chapter 15

11th Week: Ethical Leadership Methods of Rhetorical Leaders
                   Readings: Gardner, Chapters 16 and 17; Wills, Chapter 14
                   Resolving Ethical Leadership Dilemmas by Professional
                       Codes and Associations
                   Case: "The Case of the Butterfly Ballot" in Stillman,
                       Chapter 16

12th–14th Weeks: Professional Study Reports
                   Oral presentations of assigned professional studies. Twenty-
                   minute summaries and findings from this field research
                   exercise

15th–16th Weeks: Evaluation of class performance, review of oral and written
                   work, "journaling" experiences, and grades assigned by means
                   of individual student meetings with the instructor